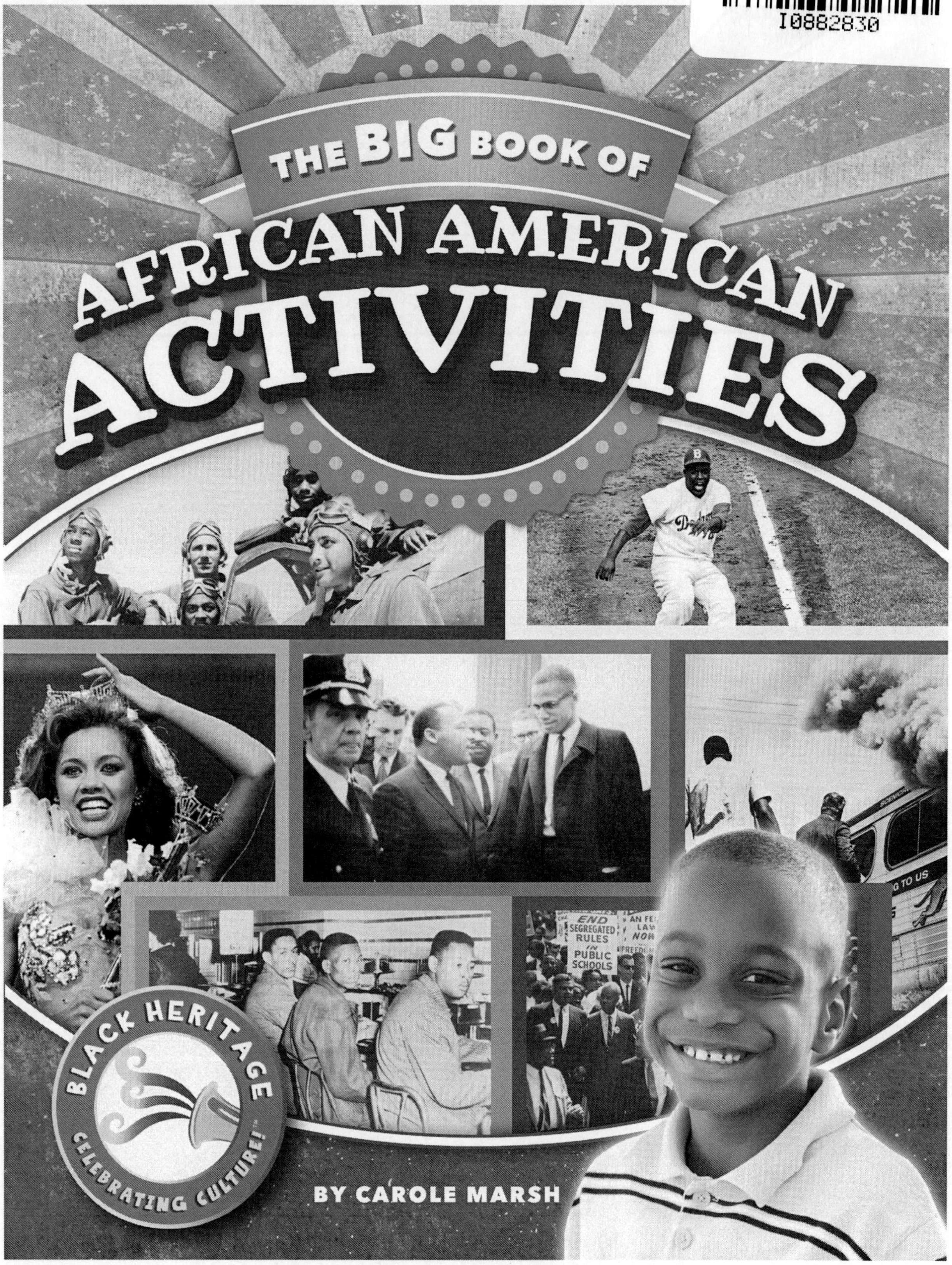
THE BIG BOOK OF
AFRICAN AMERICAN
ACTIVITIES
END SEGREGATED RULES in PUBLIC SCHOOLS
BLACK HERITAGE
CELEBRATING CULTURE!
BY CAROLE MARSH

Manufactured in Peachtree City, GA

Editorial Manager: Janice Baker • Graphic Design Manager: John Hanson

Published by

GALLOPADE

www.gallopade.com

Gallopade is proud to be a member of these educational organizations and associations:

The National School Supply and Equipment Association
The National Council for the Social Studies
Association for Supervision and Curriculum Development
Museum Store Association
Association of Partners for Public Lands

Black Heritage: Celebrating Culture Books & More!

Our Black Heritage Coloring Book

The Best Book of Black Biographies

The Big Book of African American Activities

Black Heritage GameBook: See What You Know & Learn Lots More!

Black Trivia: The African American Experience A-to-Z!

Monumental Moments in African American History

Celebrating Black Heritage:
20 Days of Activities, Reading, Recipes, Parties, Plays, and More!

African American History Timeline

Mini Timeline of Awesome African American Achievements and Events

"Let's Quilt Our African American Heritage & Stuff It Topographically!"

The Color Purple & All That Jazz!: African American Achievements in the Arts

"Out of the Mouths of Slaves": African American Oral History

The Kitchen House: How Yesterday's Black Women Created Today's Most Popular & Famous American Foods!

Black Business: African American Entrepreneurs & Their Amazing Success!

Real Kids! Real Places! Mysteries by Carole Marsh

The Mystery on the Underground Railroad

The Mystery at Motown

A Word From the Author

Dear Kids,

African American heritage is a very special history. Almost everything about African Americans is interesting and fun! This group of people shares a remarkable past that helped create the great nation of America. African Americans are unique and have accomplished many important things for our country.

This Activity Book is chock-full of activities to motivate you to learn more about African Americans. While completing puzzles, coloring activities, searching through word finds, and other fun activities, you will learn more about African American heritage, geography, history, people, places, and more.

Whether you're sitting in a classroom, riding in the backseat of a car, or doing pages for fun in your room, I hope that you have as much fun using this Activity Book as I did writing it!

Enjoy learning about African American heritage – it's the educational journey of a lifetime!

Carole Marsh

National Historic Landmarks

Use the picture clues to match each famous African American historic landmark with its name. Use the clues to help you!

African Meeting House
(known as Abolition Church)
Boston, Massachusetts
(photo 1937) ________

First Church of Christ
(enslaved people from the ship *Amistad* were educated here during their trial)
Farmington, Connecticut
(photo 1976) ________

Robert Brown Elliot School
Baltimore, Maryland
(photo 1985) ________

Culpepper Courthouse
Culpepper, Virginia
(photo 1862) ________

Martin Luther King, Jr.
(birth home)
Atlanta, Georgia
(photo 1980) ________

A

B

C

D

E

Answers: D, B, E, C, A

Black History Month!

Carter G. Woodson, an American historian, sought a way to emphasize the importance of Black history. He created Negro History Week (later to become Black History Month). Now America celebrates Black History Month every February. During this month, we focus on the contributions, sacrifices, and accomplishments of African Americans in American history. Without knowing Black history, we do not know the story of America.

Fill in each day of Black History Month with an important African American achievement or event. Some have been done already to help get you started. Celebrate each day of Black History Month by remembering these and other important contributions of African Americans!

FEBRUARY

1 Hank Aaron receives Spingarn Award for baseball achievements.	2 Hiram Revels became the first Black U.S. Senator in 1870.	3 Black Americans first met to form the NAACP in 1909.	4 Thomas Peterson was the first Black person to vote under the 15th Amendment.	5 Black statesman Frederick Douglass was born in 1817.	6	7
8	9	10	11	12	13	14
15	16	17	18	19	20	21
22	23	24	25	26	27	28

Getting to Know the Land Called Africa!

Africa is the second largest continent. It is a land filled with wildlife, grasslands, rain forests, and natural riches, such as gold and diamonds. Africa contains the world's largest desert (the Sahara) and the world's longest river (the Nile)!

1. Connect the dots with a green crayon.

2. Color the Sahara Desert red.

3. Color the Nile River blue.

4. Color the rest of Africa yellow.

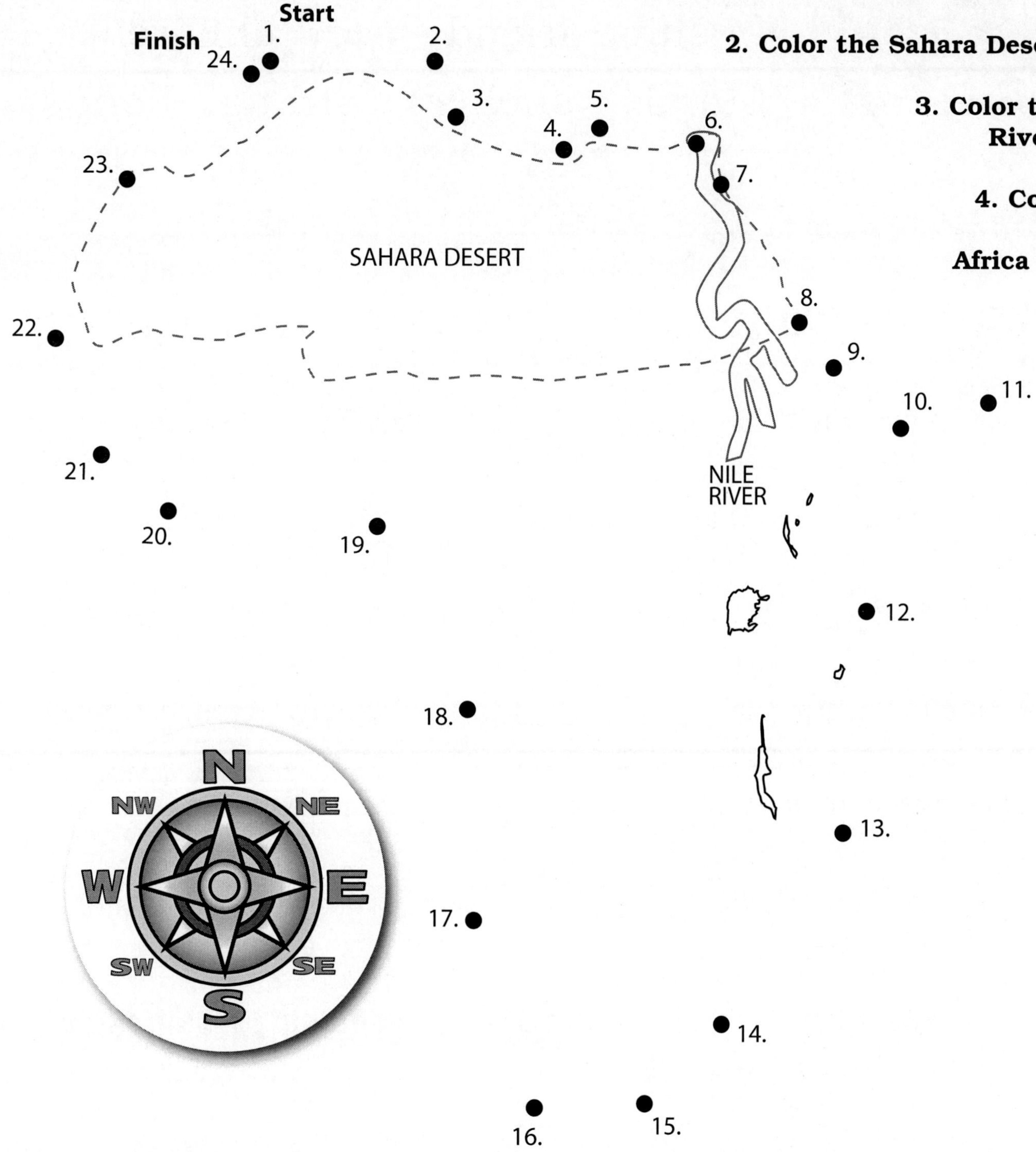

African Proverbs

Unscramble the words below! Information about the origin of each proverb is in parentheses.

WORD BANK

ship friend bed children
bundle shelters strong hands

1. To be united is to be NGSROT __________. (Africa)
2. The roof RSSTEHEL __________ the whole family. (Hausa)
3. Sticks in a UNDBLE __________ are unbreakable. (Kenya)
4. Hold a true friend with both ASNHD __________. (Nigeria)
5. CDREILNH __________ are the wisdom of the nation. (Liberia)
6. Home is a warm EBD __________ for the family. (South Africa)
7. One man cannot launch a HISP __________. (Swahili)
8. You need your FENRID __________ to help put the firewood on your back. (Zulu)

Quote

"For if one lost, all lost–the chain that held them would save all or none."
— Toni Morrison

Answers: 1. strong, 2. shelters, 3. bundle, 4. hands, 5. children, 6. bed, 7. ship, 8. friend

Who Discovered the North Pole?!

In the early 1900s, many people wanted to be the first to discover the North Pole. Explorer Robert Peary led an Arctic expedition in 1909 to find the Pole. Robert asked Matthew Henson, a Black explorer, to be his partner. The American explorers battled harsh winds and cold temperatures (as low as 60 degrees below zero!) with the help of dogs and Eskimos. The group split up to search in different directions.

Matthew Henson discovered the North Pole first! Robert asked Matthew not to speak publicly about his discovery because Matthew was a Black man. Robert was given credit for Matthew's discovery. The President even made Robert an admiral. Everyone received medals except for Matthew, even the cook! After the discovery, Matthew worked in a parking garage until some Black politicians found him a better job as a messenger. His accomplishments were not recognized until many years later.

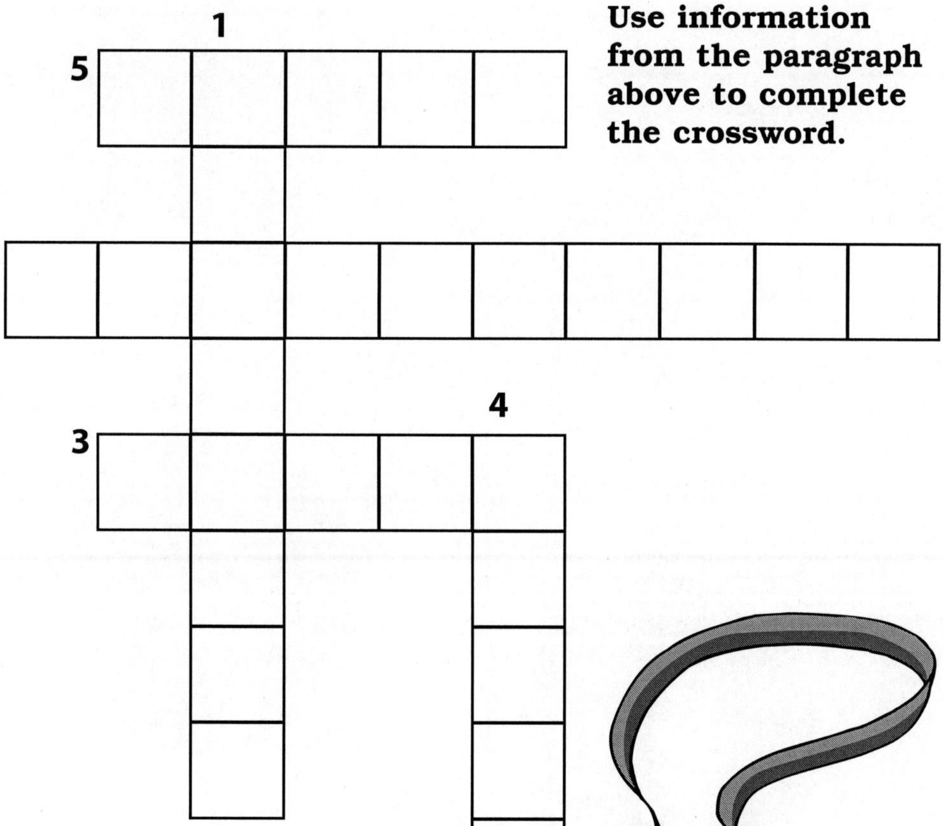

Use information from the paragraph above to complete the crossword.

1. Robert Peary was an American ______________. (DOWN)

2. Lt. Peary asked Matthew to join his Arctic ______________. (ACROSS)

3. Matthew Henson discovered the __________ Pole first! (ACROSS)

4. Lt. Peary asked Matthew __________ not to speak publicly about his discovery. (DOWN)

5. Everyone received a __________ except for Matthew, who was a Black man. (ACROSS)

Answers: 1. explorer, 2. expedition, 3. North, 4. Henson, 5. medal

Inspiring Puppets!

Cut out the faces of these inspirational Black leaders of yesterday and today. Glue them onto craft sticks. Write speeches for each puppet.

Frederick Douglass

Thurgood Marshall

Barack Obama

Sojourner Truth

Martin Luther King, Jr.

Booker T. Washington

Rosa Parks

Have a puppet parade!

One Small Step... One Giant Leap!

African American astronauts made leaps and bounds in the NASA program. Their contributions launched new steps into space for America.

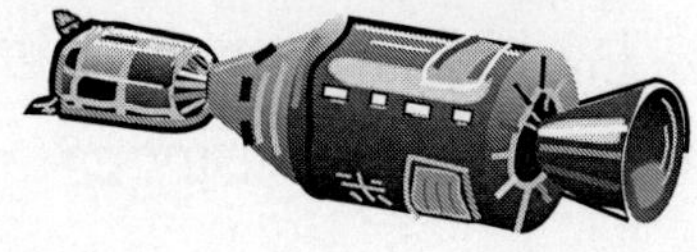

ASTRONAUT	SPACECRAFT	WOW!	DATE
1. Mae Jemison	Endeavor	first Black woman in space!	1992
2. Frederick Gregory	Discovery	first Black Space Commander!	1989
3. Charles Bolden	Discovery	helped launch Hubble space telescope!	1990
4. Guion Bluford	Challenger	first African American in space!	1983
5. Bernard Harris	Discovery	first African American to walk in space!	1995
6. Ronald McNair	Challenger	second African American in space!	1984
7. Joan Higginbotham	Discovery	first mission with two Black astronauts!	2006
8. Winston Scott	Endeavor	performed gravity experiment in space!	1996

Put the above years into chronological order. Then write them in that order on the planets (1-8) around the universe. Use the blanks.

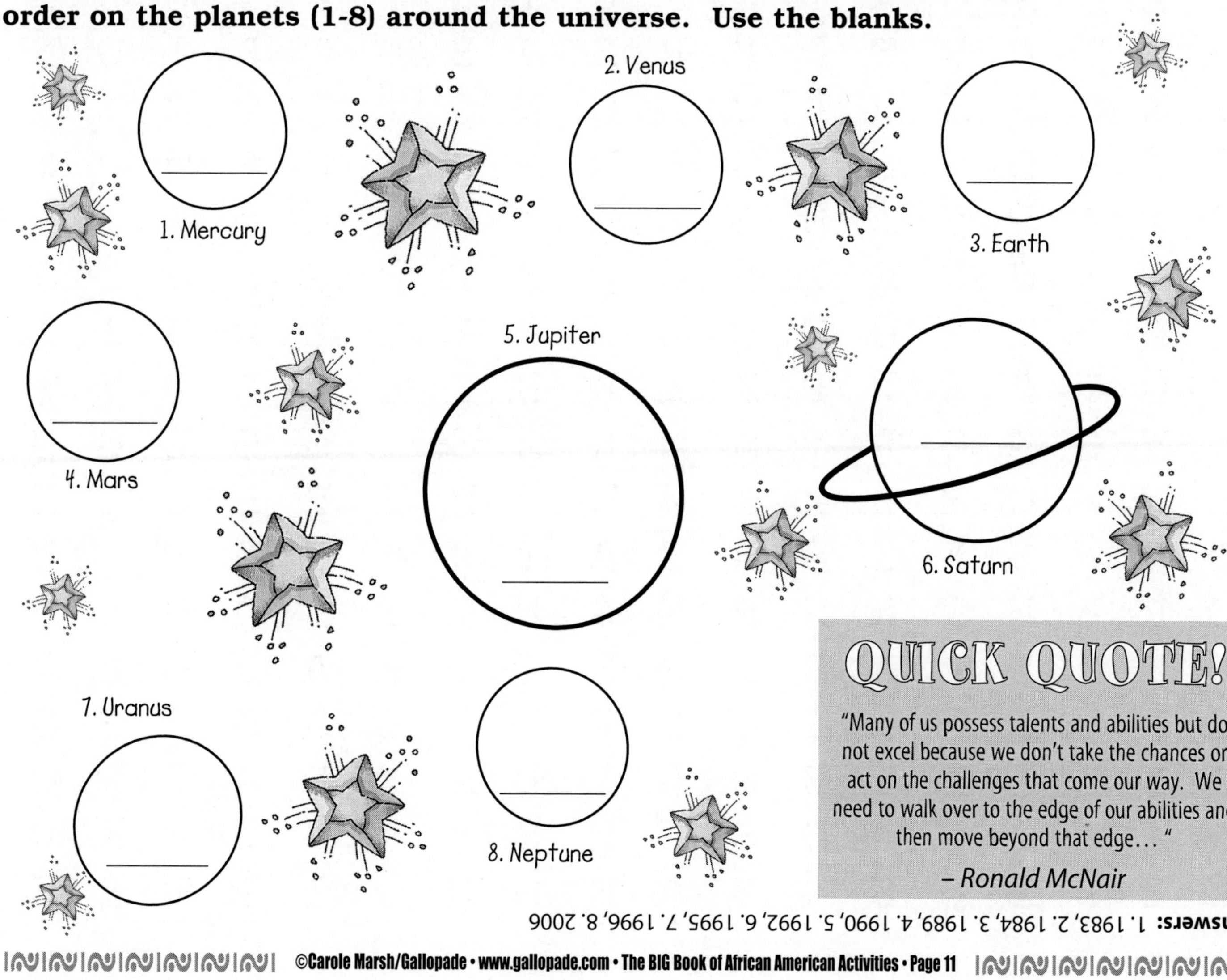

QUICK QUOTE!

"Many of us possess talents and abilities but do not excel because we don't take the chances or act on the challenges that come our way. We need to walk over to the edge of our abilities and then move beyond that edge..."

– Ronald McNair

Answers: 1. 1983, 2. 1984, 3. 1989, 4. 1990, 5. 1992, 6. 1995, 7. 1996, 8. 2006

Jazzy, Pizzazzy, Razzamatazzy Word Search

Jazz music developed in African American communities across the United States. The words below include legendary singers and musicians, and famous jazz hotspots.

Find the words.

WORD BANK

Ella Fitzgerald	Duke Ellington	Billie Holiday
Louis Armstrong	Fletcher Henderson	Dizzy Gillespie
Fats Waller	Jelly Roll Morton	Greenwich Village
Cotton Club	Harlem	Queens
New Orleans	Memphis	South Chicago

F L E T C H E R H E N D E R S O N D
D A Q P G R O G A C I H C H T U O S
U K T U R T D F R E J B F T Z I D N
K N S S E H B U L C N O T T O C E K
E I B O W E E M E M P H I S K W D E
E T A P E A N F M I Z A R C O P I A
L F E J G R L S C P Z T H R S J Z J
L N O T R O M L L O R Y L L E J Z F
I O T E S X P K E K H E E I E O Y T
N V G N O R T S M R A S I U O L G G
G V W O Y Z Z A V N N R F P A U I H
T C W E F I J N S A I N H E N T L B
O R A N T W S P E G E C T S Q U L P
N F S D L A R E G Z T I F A L L E F
G R E E N W I C H V I L L A G E S Q
B I L L I E H O L I D A Y P A F P C
N I L L Q A O S C L S Y E Y U L I U
X Z L B Q S L Y A E M M O I P M E S

Women in Government

In 2020, Kamala Harris was elected as the first female, African American, and Asian American Vice President of the United States. Kamala was born in Oakland, California. She graduated from Howard University and then attended law school at the University of California, Hastings College of the Law.

She worked for the government in California. She was a district attorney in San Francisco. Then, she became the attorney general of California. After that, she became a U.S. Senator! When she was elected to become Vice President, she said "While I may be the first woman in this office, I will not be the last." Who do you think will be NEXT?

Unscramble the last names of the first female Black Americans to hold each of these roles in our government.

1. Secretary of State AND National Security Advisor

   Condoleezza ____________ EIRC

2. U.S. Senator

   Carol Moseley ____________________ RABUN

3. U.S. Congresswoman

   Shirley _________________________ MSIHHOCL

Answers: 1. Rice, 2. Braun, 3. Chisholm

"Let's Play Hide and Seek!"

In 2008, Barack Obama was elected as the first African American President of the United States. Presidents and their families live in the White House in Washington, D.C. Since the White House has 134 rooms, there were plenty of places for the President's children to play hide and seek! Use the Word Bank to label the following hiding spots!

WORD BANK

Blue Room **China Room** **East Room** **Library** **Lincoln Bedroom** **Map Room**
Oval Office **Queens' Bedroom** **Situation Room** **Press Room**

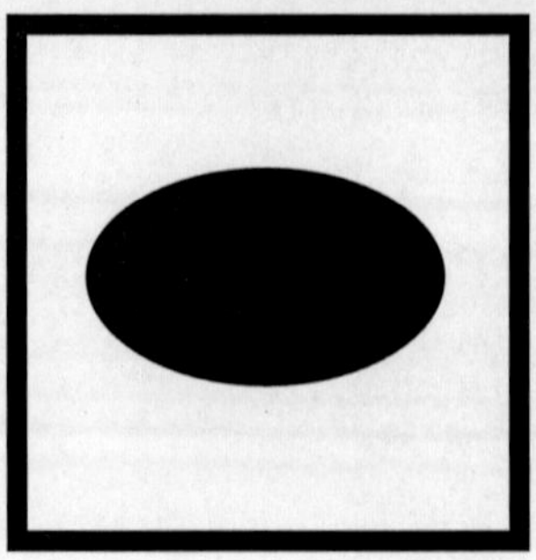

Let It Wave!

Marcus Garvey, a famous African American leader, created a new flag for Black people in the early 1900s. This new flag was called a bendera. A red stripe at the top symbolizes the difficult struggle for freedom and equality. A black stripe in the middle represents unity and encourages the Black community to stay together. The green stripe stands for the future!

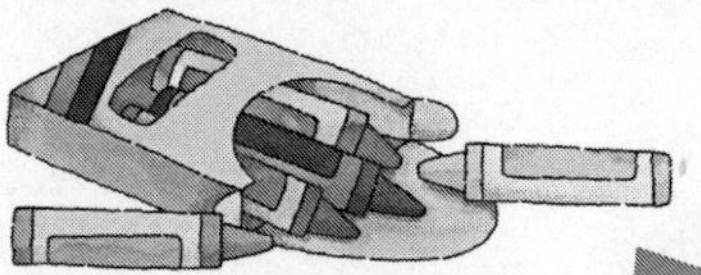

Color the bendera flag!

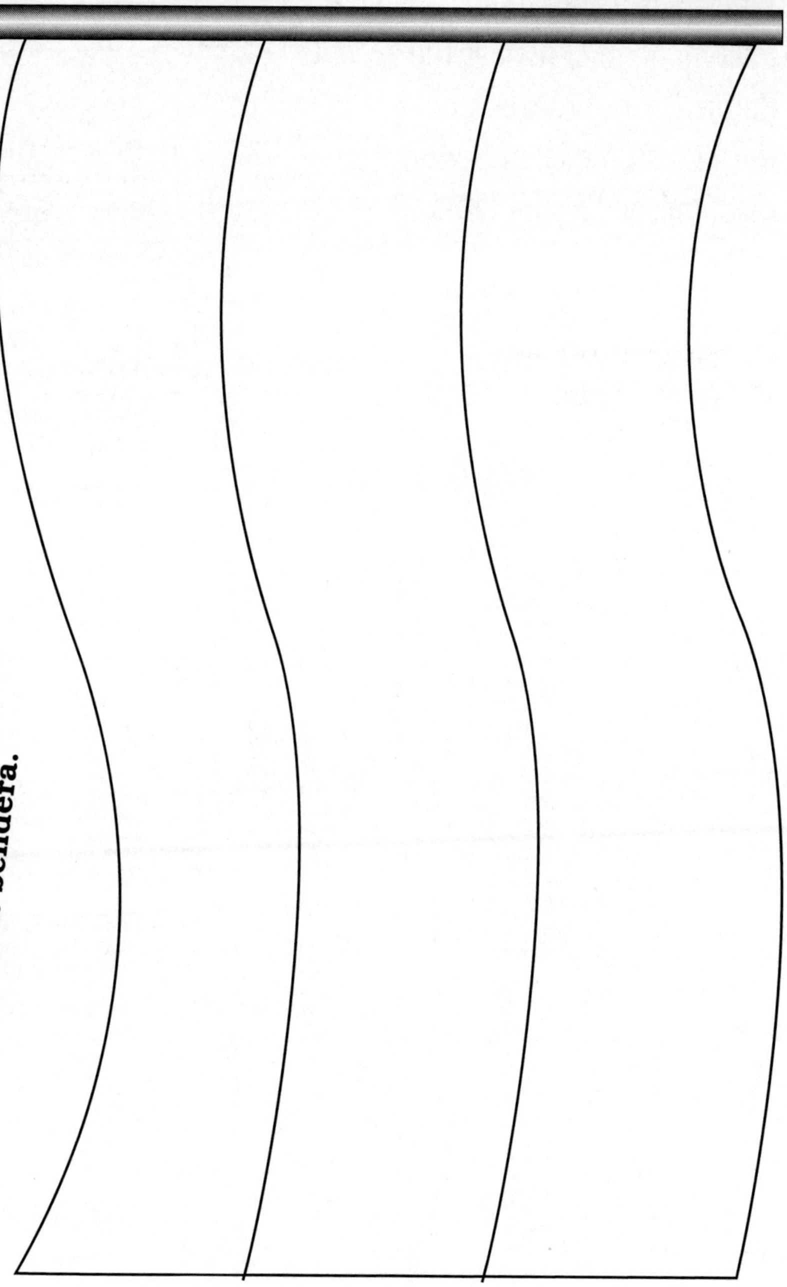

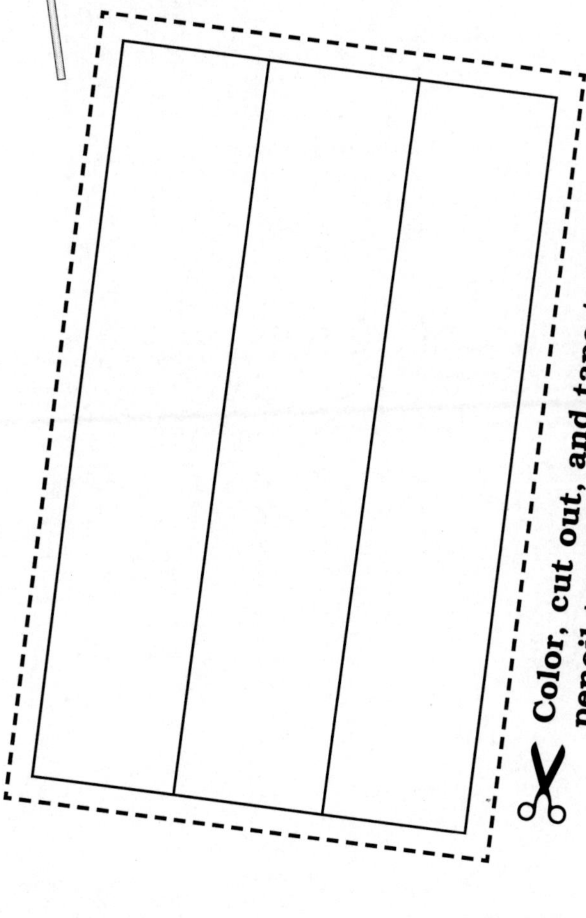

Color, cut out, and tape to your pencil to make a bendera.

Medals of Honor

African Americans have served our country bravely in many wars, including the American Revolution and the Civil War. Several African Americans have earned military honors, such as the Purple Heart, Bronze Star, Navy Cross, Medal of Honor, Distinguished Flying Cross, and others.

Color and cut out these medals.

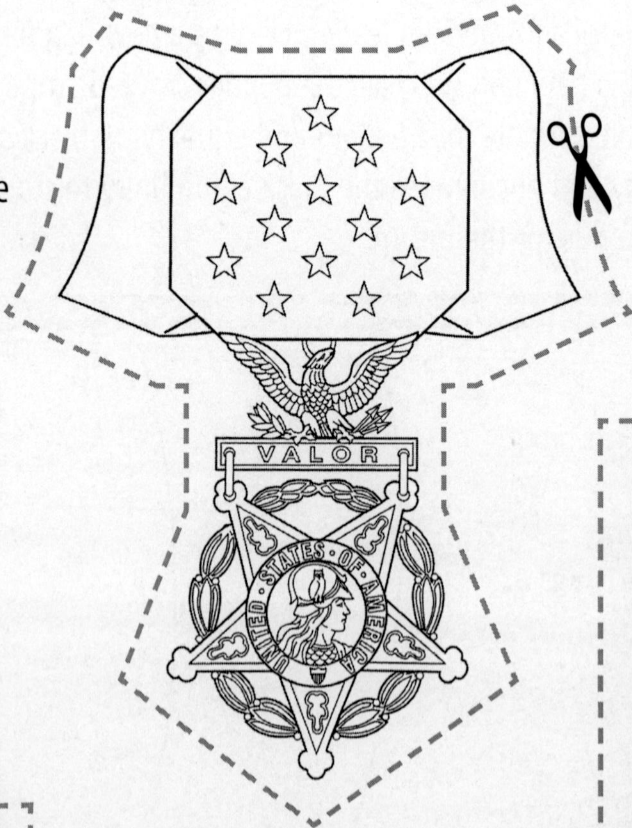

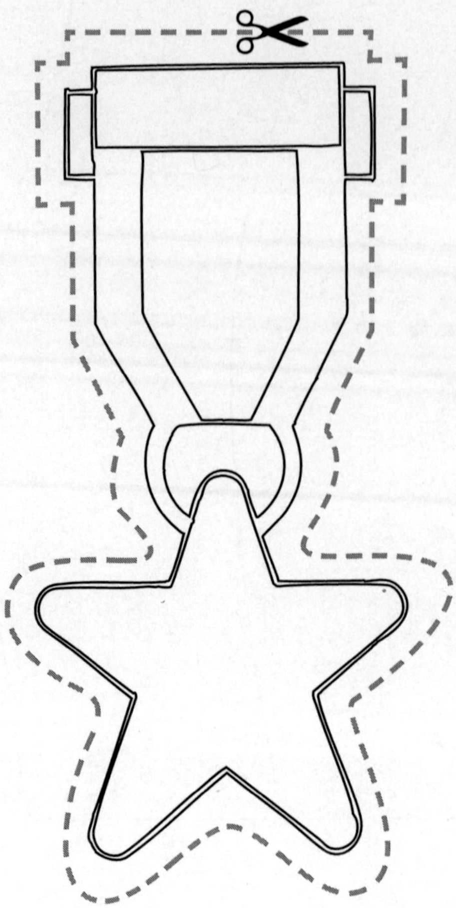

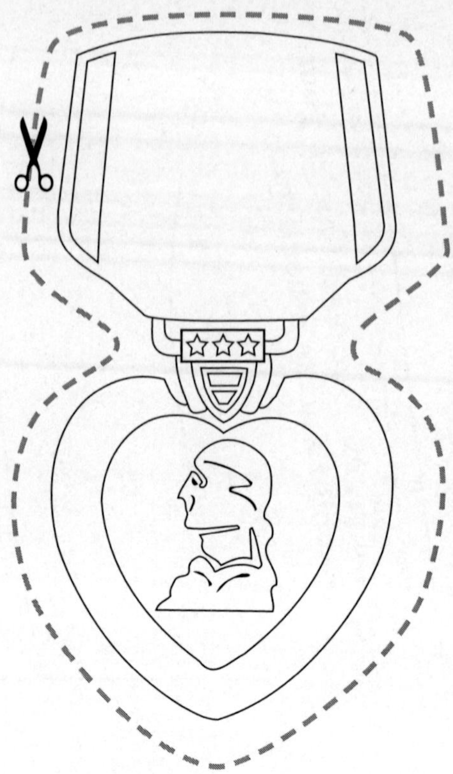

Continuing an Oral Tradition!

Most enslaved people were not allowed to learn how to read and write. They passed down their history by singing spirituals and telling stories. Many cultures have practiced this oral form of communication, and some still do today!

Ask an older African American for an interview. Perhaps you could talk with a grandparent, a friend, or a teacher! Ask this person some of the questions below. Ask some of your own questions too! Think about your interview. What new things did you learn?

1. Where and when were you born? Describe your hometown.
2. What were your parents like? What did they teach you?
3. Please describe some experiences from your school days.
4. What were some of your favorite things to do when you were growing up?
5. Did you ever experience discrimination because of your race?

6. ____

7. ____

Write a short paragraph (at least 3-4 sentences!) that tells the story of the person that you interviewed.

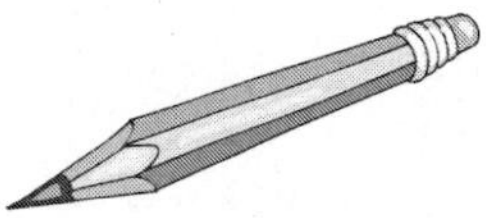

____

____

____

____

____

____

____

Listening + Doing + Thinking = Learning

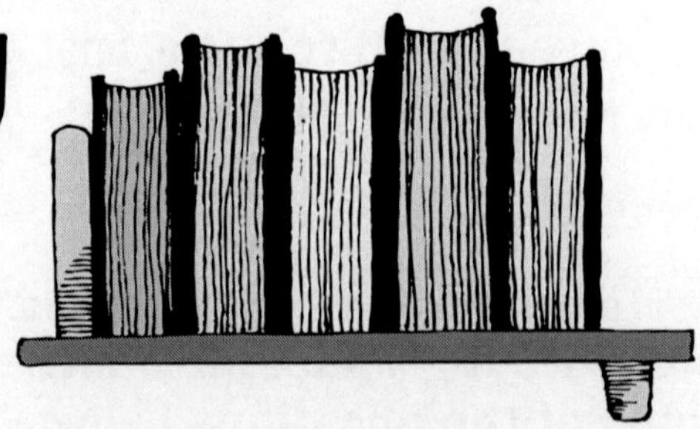

Complete the math problems to discover what year these amazing academic achievements occurred.

1. Richard Theodore Greener is the first African American to graduate from Harvard University.
   600 + 475 + 125 – 45 + 395 + 455 + 25 – 160 = ________

2. African American Booker T. Washington leads Tuskegee Institute.
   550 + 325 + 650 – 90 + 225 + 900 - 400 – 279 = ________

3. African American Fanny Jackson Coppins starts a school for African American students.
   100 + 875 + 505 – 120 + 425 + 600 - 425 – 72 = ________

4. African American Mary McLeod Bethune founds a Black college.
   125 + 240 + 775 – 30 + 635 + 720 - 400 – 161 = ________

5. Alain Leroy Locke is the first African American Rhodes Scholar.
   195 + 780 + 435 – 60 + 75 + 845 -300 – 63 = ________

6. Eva Beatrice Dykes is the first African American woman to finish her Ph.D. requirements.
   55 + 895 + 200 – 20 + 715 + 125 + 25 – 74 = ________

7. Six-year-old Ruby Bridges is the first Black child to desegregate a white school.
   90 + 45 + 880 – 75 + 495 + 525 + 80 – 80 = ________

Answers: 1. 1870, 2. 1881, 3. 1888, 4. 1904, 5. 1907, 6. 1921, 7. 1960

Set Us Free!

The Emancipation Proclamation of 1863 declared that all enslaved people living in states that had rebelled against the Union were free!

Draw a circle around the president who issued the Emancipation Proclamation. Color the presidents.

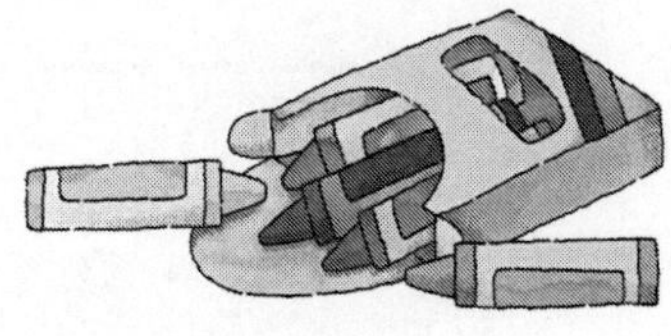

Abraham Lincoln

John F. Kennedy

Franklin D. Roosevelt

Barack Obama

George Washington

Thomas Jefferson

Answer: Abraham Lincoln

Business Code Buster

Solve the codes to find out the names of some successful African American businesspeople.

CODE KEY

A	B	C	D	E	F	G	H	I	J	K	L	M
✹	❁	✣	♣	➳	❤	❢	✲	✄	✆	☛	✈	✉

N	O	P	Q	R	S	T	U	V	W	X	Y	Z
✿	☆	✦	✡	✎	❦	☎	✒	✚	✖	✍	✠	✓

1. ___ ___ ___ ___ ___ "___ ___ ___ ___"
✖ ✹ ✈ ✈ ✠ ✹ ✉ ☆ ❦
___ ___ ___ ___ ___ ___ ___
❤ ☆ ✎ ☎ ✒ ✿ ➳

2. ___ ___ ___ ___ ___ ___ ___
✈ ➳ ☆ ✿ ✹ ✎ ♣
___ ___ ___ ___ ___ ___
❢ ☆ ✈ ♣ ➳ ✿

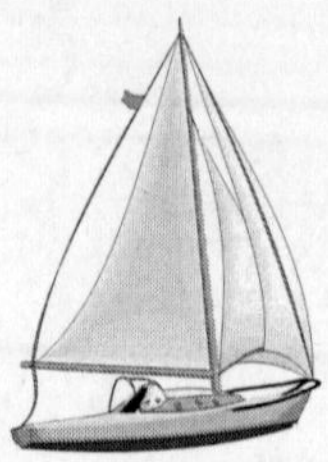

3. ___ ___ ___ ___ ___
✆ ✹ ✉ ➳ ❦
___ ___ ___ ___ ___ ___, ___ ___.
❤ ☆ ✎ ☎ ➳ ✿ ❦ ✎

4. ___ ___ ___ ___ ___ ___ ___. ___.
✉ ✹ ♣ ✹ ✉ ➳ ✣ ✆
___ ___ ___ ___ ___ ___
✖ ✹ ✈ ☛ ➳ ✎

Answers: 1. Wally Amos Fortune, 2. Leonard Golden, 3. James Forten, Sr., 4. Madame C.J. Walker

At Last, At Last... Free at Last!

The Emancipation Proclamation

President Abraham Lincoln delivered the Emancipation Proclamation on January 1, 1863 during the Civil War. He said that enslaved people in the rebelling states were free! That meant that slavery was finally illegal there. Slavery was one of the main reasons why Northern and Southern states fought each other. More than 200,000 Black men joined the Union army to fight. Almost 40,000 Black soldiers died serving their country in the Civil War.

Juneteenth celebrates the ending of slavery in ALL of the U.S. after the Civil War.

Use the Word Bank to fill in the sentence blanks.

WORD BANK

1863	Civil	freed
Union	40,000	Lincoln

1. The Emancipation Proclamation _______________ enslaved people in the rebelling states!

2. During the Civil War, many Black men fought in the _______________ Army.

3. Nearly _________________ Black soldiers died in the Civil War.

4. The ____________ War was fought between the North and South.

5. President Abraham _____________ delivered the Emancipation Proclamation in January of _______.

FAST FACT

Black people suffered discrimination even in the Union Army! Black soldiers received $7 monthly pay, but white soldiers were paid $13 a month. Black soldiers strongly protested against the unfair pay rate. Congress changed the law in 1864 to require that all soldiers receive equal pay.

Answers: 1. freed, 2. Union, 3. 40,000, 4. Civil, 5. Lincoln, 1863

African American Spelling Bee!

Good spelling is a good habit!

Study the words on the page. Most all of them can be found within the activities in this book! Then fold the right half of the page under. Take a "spelling test!" Ask a friend to read the words aloud to you. Write the correct spelling on the line. When finished, unfold the page and check your spelling. How many did you spell right? Study the words you miss.

WORDS:

freedom
leader
Africa
escape
jazz
King
discrimination
poet
ship
Tuskegee
Black
emancipation
proclamation
boycott
Olympian
civil rights

Streeeeeeetch!

"Pull apart" these sentences to find out some cool trivia about African Americans! Write your answer on the lines provided.

1. WilliamAlexanderLeidesdorffwasthefirstAfricanAmericanmillionaire andthefirstknownBlackdiplomatintheUnitedStates.

2. DorieMillerwasawardedtheNavyCrossforhisheroismduringthePearl Harborattack.

3. MichelleObamaworkedasalawyerbeforebecomingFirstLadyof theUnitedStates.

4. LieutenantGeneralBenjaminO.DavisJr.,aWestPointgraduate,became thefirstBlackAirForcegeneralin1954.

Quilting Bee!

Enslaved women created quilts to tell their life stories for decades. Their quilts encouraged friendship, provided comfort and beauty, and expressed joy or sadness. The art of quilt making has survived time, technology, and changing fashion.

Think about the most important events of your life. Perhaps your first day of school or when you won a special award! Maybe the day your family welcomed a new brother or sister. Don't forget your first birthday! Draw colorful picture that represents each event - in order - inside the nine quilt squares. Use the last square to illustrate the future! You will create a beautiful story quilt of your life!

Symbol Scramble

Write the correct number next to each item related to African American history.

___ Tuskegee Airmen patch ___ Black History Month ___ kente cloth

___ jazz musician's trumpet ___ Spingarn Medal ___ Poet Maya Angelou's pen

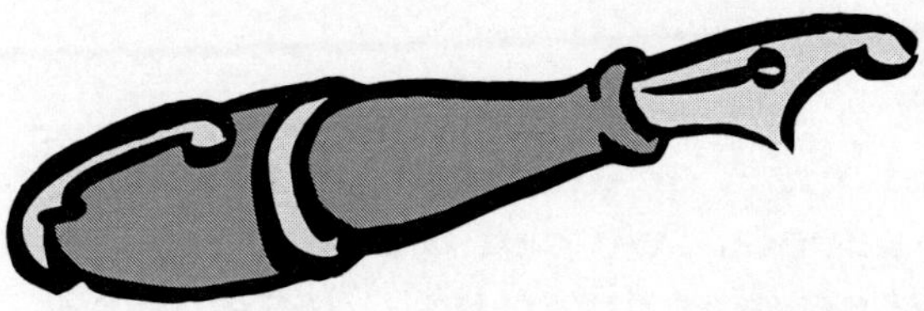

3

4

6

2

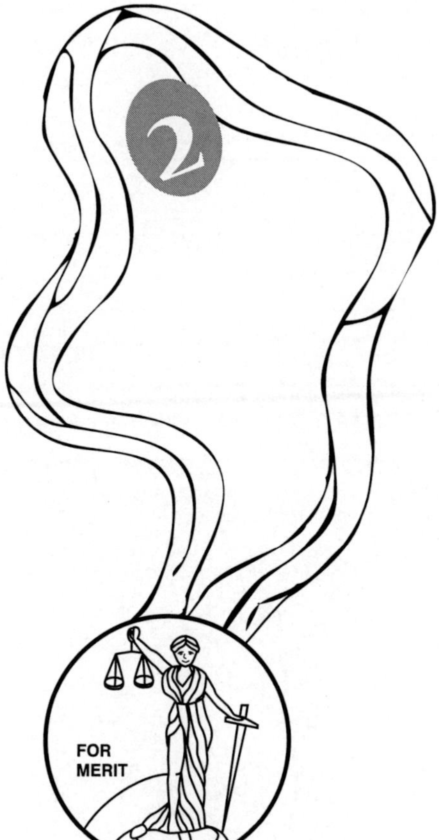

5

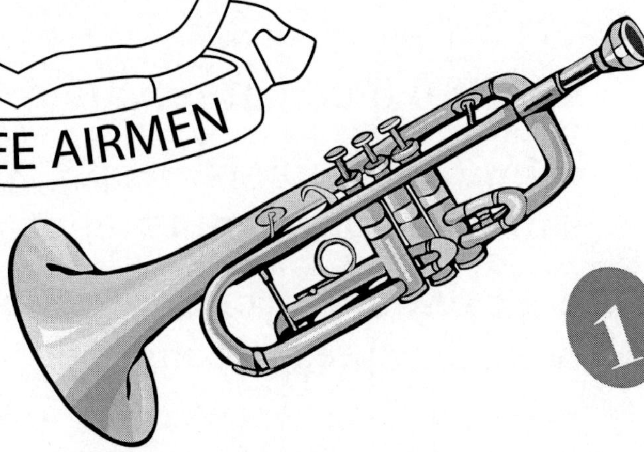

1

Embrace African Heritage!

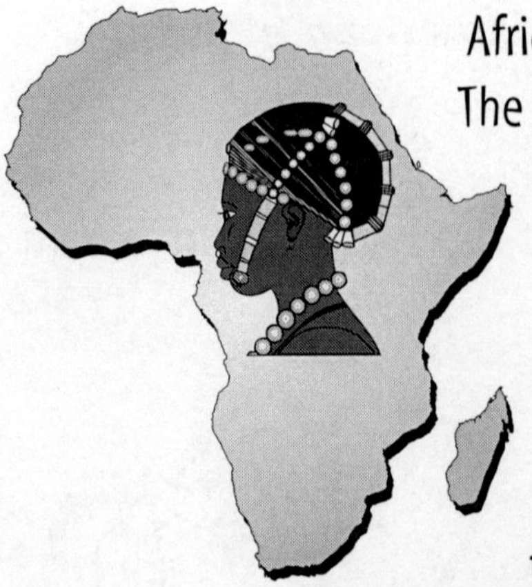

Africa hosts one of the world's most diverse collection of people and cultures. The land is rich in natural resources, wildlife, and ethnic heritage. Africa is the second largest continent in the world and the only one to exist in all hemispheres. Aside from the mountains (Kilimanjaro) and deserts (Sahara), the terrain is a grassy home to a greater range of animals than in any other part of the world.

America benefits from the diverse, or different, ethnic origins that make up the American people. We can learn about each other's heritage. In this way, we share our diversity. Name one example for each category below that represents your heritage!

1. Holiday: ______________________
2. Food: ______________________
3. Clothing: ______________________
4. Religion: ______________________
5. Music: ______________________
6. Economy: ______________________
7. Wildlife: ______________________
8. Military: ______________________
9. Attraction: ______________________

diverse: different or varied

ethnic: a group of people who have the same language, culture, or religion

custom: a way of doing something that has been accepted among a group of people

Places to Go! Things to Do!

African Americans have left their mark all over our great nation. There are lots of fun places to visit in America where you can learn more about Black heritage and accomplishments.

Match the cities with their states by drawing a line to connect them!

- The Civil Rights Institute, Birmingham
- Museum of the National Center of Afro-American Artists, Boston
- Amistad Research Center, New Orleans
- Tuskegee Airmen National Museum, Detroit
- Martin Luther King, Jr. National Historic Site, Atlanta
- Black American West Museum & Heritage Center, Denver
- National Civil Rights Museum, Memphis
- Greensboro Historical Museum, Greensboro
- African American Museum of Fine Arts, San Diego

Answers: Alabama, Massachusetts, Louisiana, Michigan, Georgia, Colorado, Tennessee, North Carolina, California

African Americans in Government Hunt!

Many African Americans serve as public servants in the U.S. government. Their jobs are very important because they help make sure our country stays safe and free!

Below is a list of some African Americans who have served or are serving in U.S. government. Go on a scavenger hunt and research one fact about each person such as a job title, award, or special accomplishment. Use an encyclopedia, almanac, library book, the Internet, or even an expert!

General Colin Powell ___U.S Secretary of State___

Hon. Clarence Thomas ______________________

Senator J.C. Watts ______________________

Condoleezza Rice ______________________

Dr. Ralph Bunche ______________________

Jefferson Long ______________________

Harold Ford, Jr. ______________________

David Dinkins ______________________

John M. Langston ______________________

Charles Hayes ______________________

Rod Paige ______________________

John Lewis ______________________

Robert Smalls ______________________

Bobby Rush ______________________

Thurgood Marshall ______________________

Harold Washington ______________________

Barack Obama ______________________

L. Douglas Wilder ______________________

Shirley Chisholm ______________________

Proud to Be an African American!

The basic principles of our government require that all Americans are entitled to enjoy the rights of life, liberty, and the pursuit of happiness; and equality before the law.

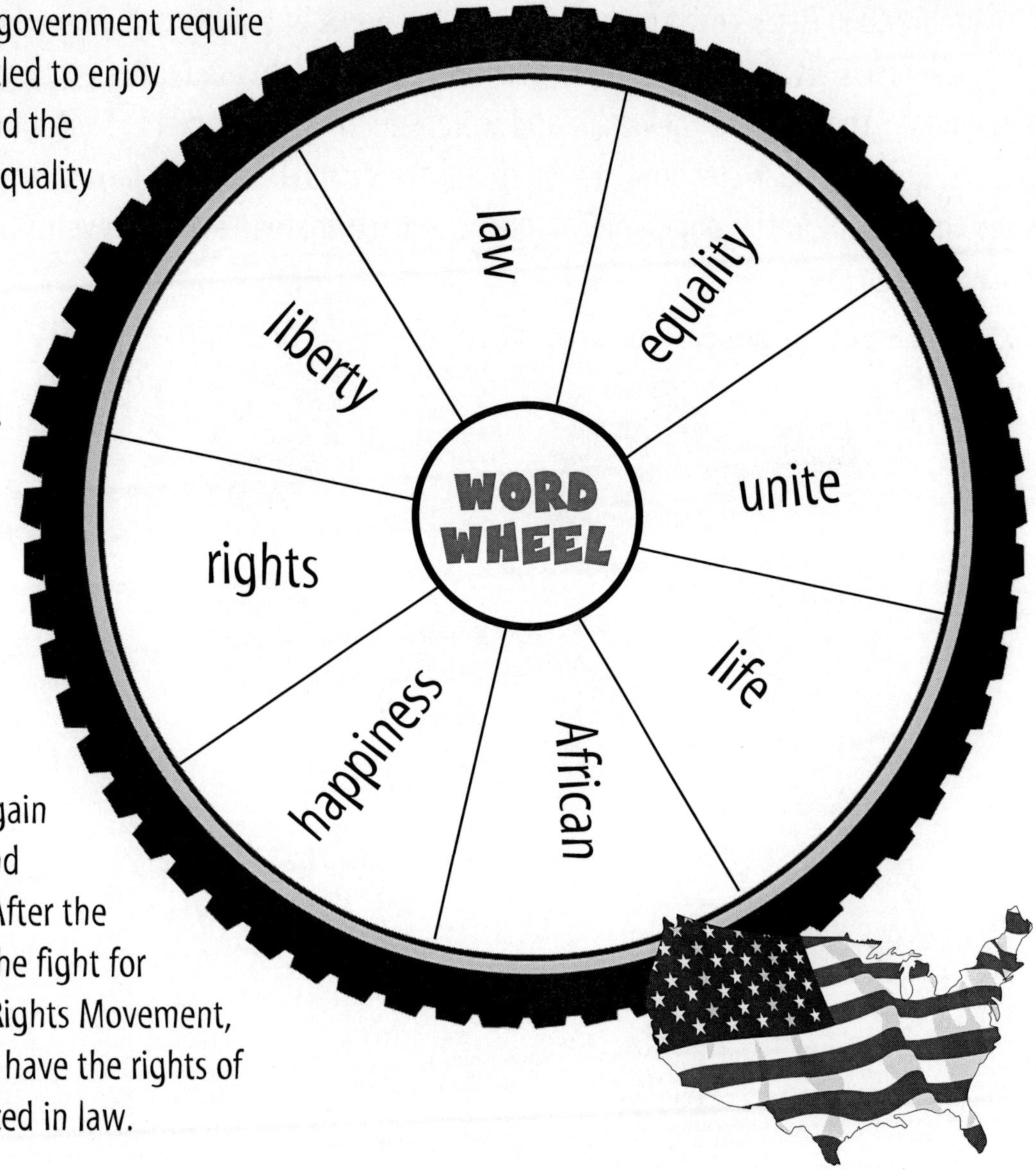

Throughout American history, African Americans have fought for their rights as Americans! Already free Black Americans fought to free enslaved Black people before the Civil War.

Many Black Americans fought IN the Civil War to gain the rights of life, liberty, and the pursuit of happiness. After the Civil War, they continued the fight for equality. During the Civil Rights Movement, many Americans fought to have the rights of African Americans recognized in law.

Read the paragraph. Use the Word Wheel to fill in the blanks.

________________ Americans have fought for their ________________ as Americans throughout our history. Individual rights to ______________, ______________, and the pursuit of ______________________; and ________________ under the __________ are the basic principles that form the United States government. These are the principles that ____________________ all Americans.

Answers: African, rights, life, liberty, happiness, equality, law, unite

Riding, Roping, and Rodeos!

About 9,000 Black cowboys helped drive big herds of cattle West after the Civil War. Even though they still faced discrimination, these Black workers were treated more equally on the range than elsewhere. They proved their skills and were valued ranch workers. Skills mattered to the rancher bosses, and the Black cowboys proved themselves valuable on the ranch. Then Black cowboys used those skills in the popular local rodeos to participate in exciting events like riding bulls and bucking broncos!

Label the rodeo gear. Use the Word Bank.

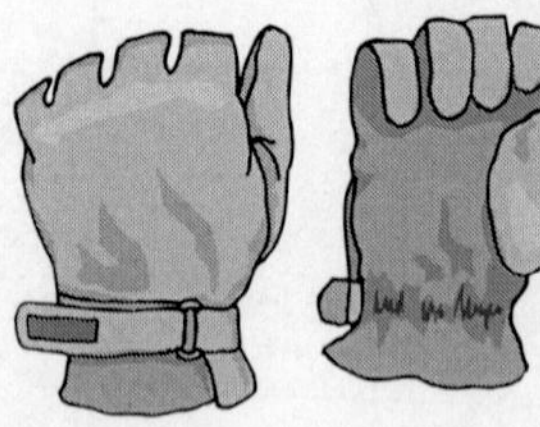

______

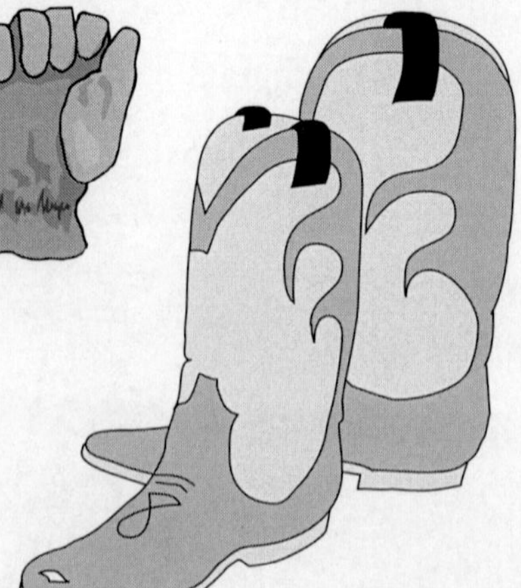

______

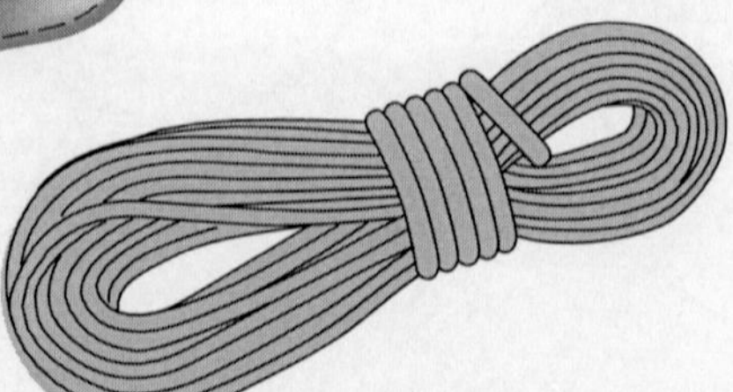

______

______

WORD BANK

spurs	chaps
vest	boots
lariat	hat
gloves	saddle

______

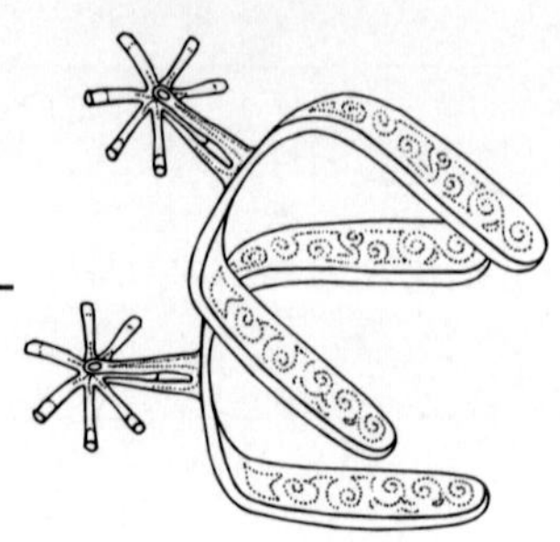

______

______

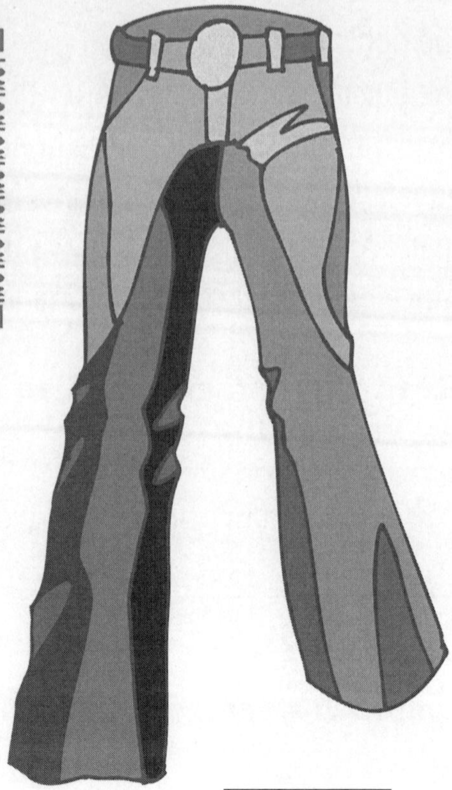

______

What a Great Idea!

Inventors watch how things work in the world. They think about how to make things better. Their ideas help make the world safer, easier, or more efficient. Many Black inventors have improved people's lives with their creative inventions. Complete the activity below to find out more about a few of the most famous Black inventors.

Match each inventor with the correct invention. Use the picture clues!

INVENTOR	INVENTION
____ Garrett Morgan 	A. Lubrication for Steam Engine
____ Henry Blair 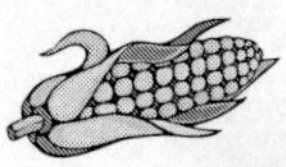	B. Traffic Light
____ Jan Matzeliger 	C. Electric Light Bulb Filament
____ Lewis Latimer 	D. Wooden Clock
____ Elijah McCoy 	E. Shoe Sole Sewing Machine
____ Joseph Winters 	F. Bicycle Basket
____ Granville Woods 	G. Golf Tee
____ Jerry Certain 	H. Big Blue Mailbox (public use)
____ Benjamin Banneker 	I. Railway Telegraph
____ George Grant 	J. Fire Escape Ladder
____ Phillip Downing 	K. Corn Planter
____ John Albert Burr 	L. Lawnmower (device to keep grass from clogging gears)

Answers: B, K, E, C, A, J, I, F, D, G, H, L

Soul Food

Hundreds of years ago, enslaved women did most of the cooking for white families, especially in the South. They creatively used spices from nature and invented new recipes that were often inspired by foods from their original homelands. Many of these recipes are now known as "soul food." People across the U.S. enjoy these foods today!

WORDBANK

sweet potato pone	okra	succotash	sassafras
collards	black-eyed peas	hominy	fried chicken
cornbread	cabbage	red-eye gravy	grits
benne seeds	pecan pie	peaches	boiled peanuts
chitlins	molasses	yam pudding	gumbo

Use the Word Bank of recipes and ingredients to complete the crossword puzzle.

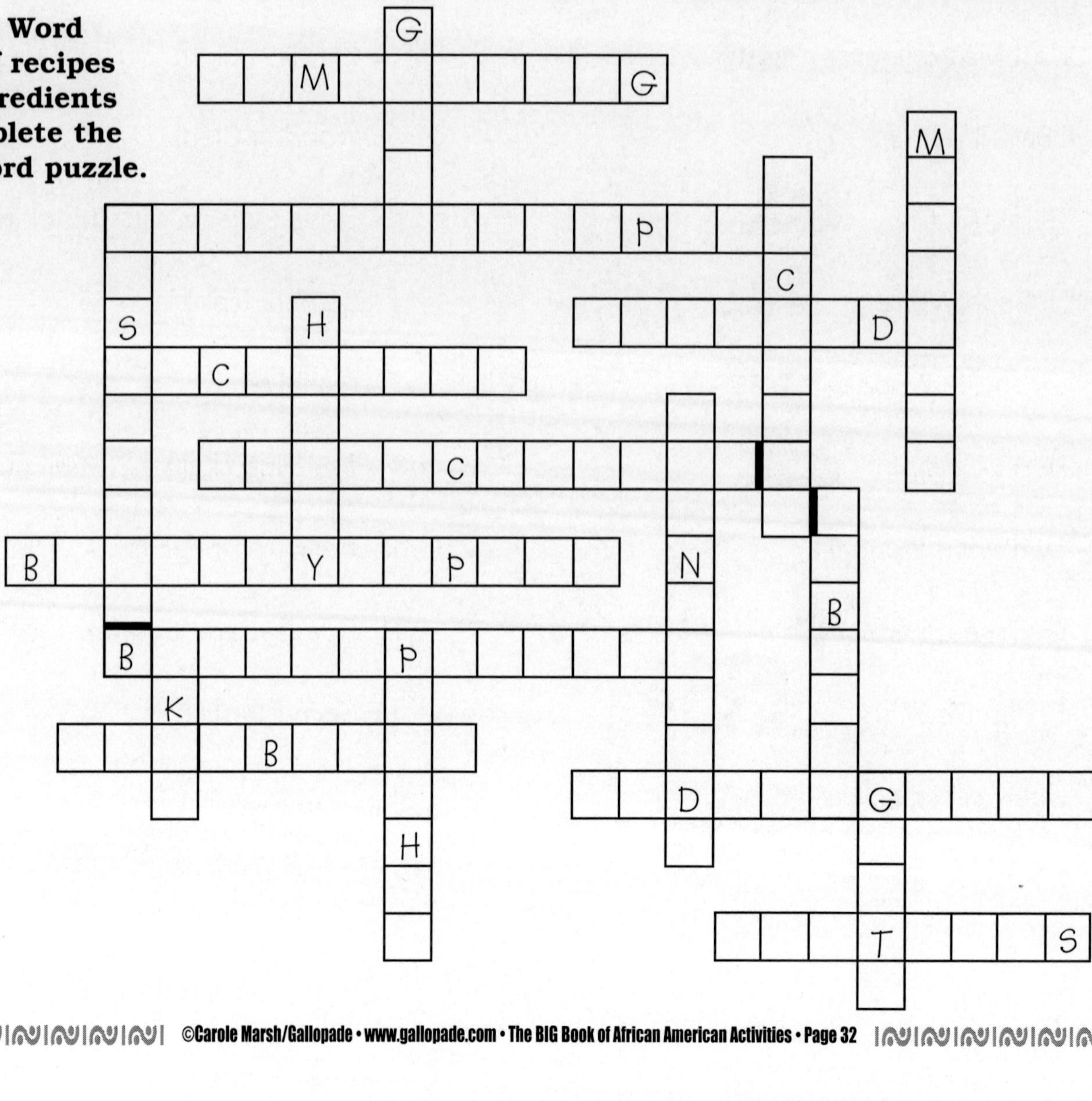

Tracing our Roots!

The ancestors of most Americans came to the United States from somewhere else. Many of the ancestors of African Americas were enslaved and forced to come to America. Some African Americans trace their roots to find out where in Africa their ancestors lived.

Use a red crayon to trace a path through the maze from the United States map to Africa. Color Africa green. Color the United States blue.

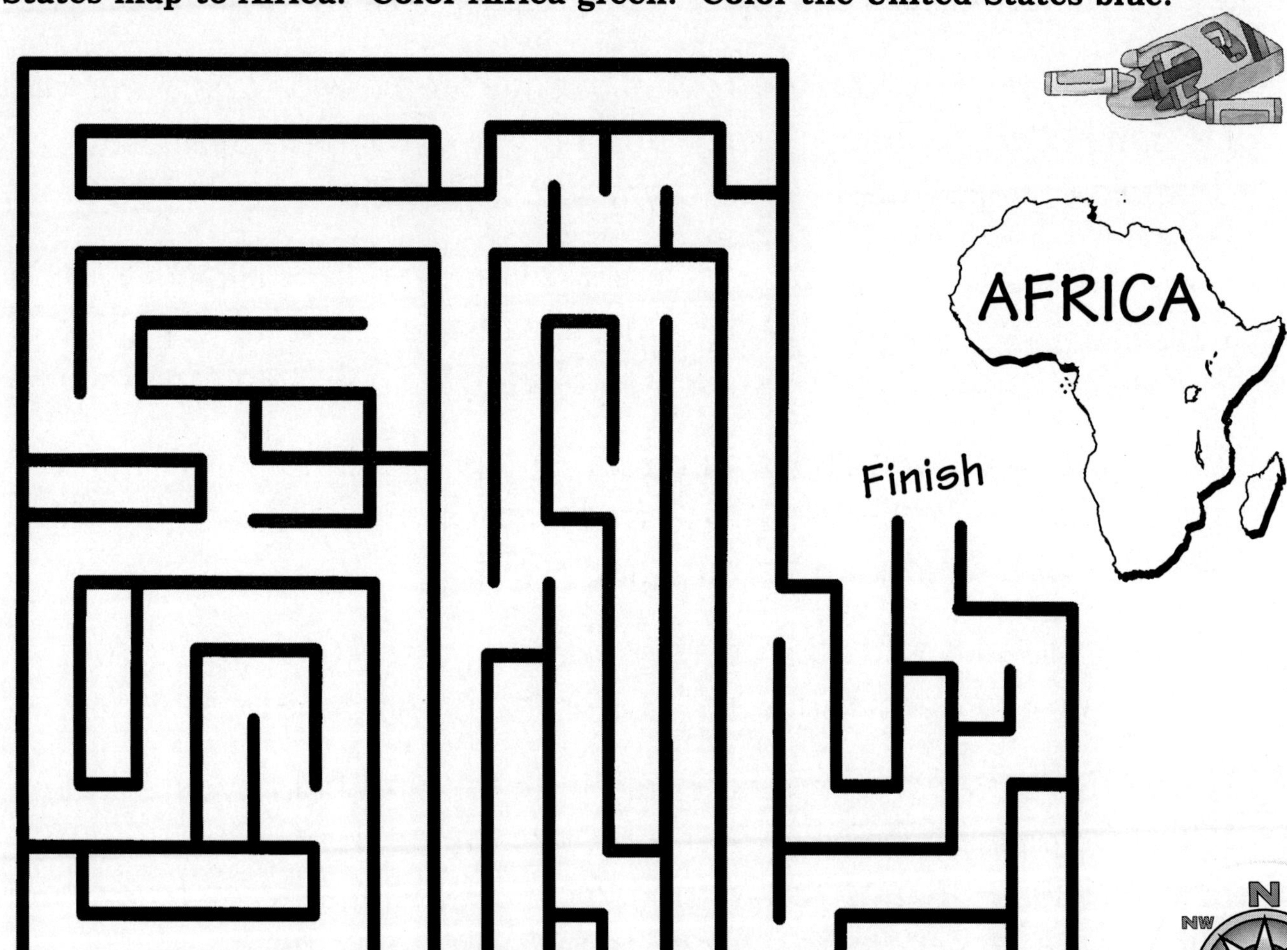

Amazing Olympic Athletes!

Have you ever dreamed of winning a medal in the international Olympic Games? African American athletes have brought several Olympic medals home to America over the years! Many Black athletes have also made America proud by breaking world records at the Olympic events!

Number the Olympic medalists in the correct order, ending with the most recent year.

______ Carl Lewis is one of only 4 Olympic athletes to win 9 gold medals. He competed in several track and field events in 4 separate Olympic Games. Carl's last Olympic competition was in **1996**.

______ Florence Griffith-Joyner won 3 gold medals at the **1988** Olympic Games. She also won 2 silver medals in the previous Olympics. Florence's fans nicknamed her Flojo and would cheer "Go Flo!"

______ Gabby Douglas won the gold medal in the Individual All-Around gymnastics event at the **2012** Summer Olympics, becoming the first African American to win that event.

______ Simone Biles won a total of five medals at the **2016** Olympics! She won four gold medals and one bronze in gymnastics events.

______ Wilma Rudolph won 3 gold medals in track and field events in the **1960** Olympics. She also won a bronze medal in her first Olympic competition – at age 16! Wilma overcame polio, scarlet fever, and pneumonia to become an American Olympic heroine!

______ Jesse Owens broke 5 world records in track and field events during the **1936** Olympic Games. He won 4 gold medals!

______ In **2002**, Vonetta Flowers became the first African American to win an Olympic gold medal in the Winter Games. She was part of a two-woman bobsleigh team.

Answers: 4, 3, 6, 7, 2, 1, 5

Carver's Treats!

George Washington Carver is remembered as one of America's greatest scientists. This African American farming wizard figured out how to create more than 300 products from peanuts, and many products from sweet potatoes and pecans, too! Carver also directed the agricultural department at Tuskegee Industrial Institute in Alabama. He told farmers to plant different crops each year to help put nutrients back into the soil. Carver's discoveries and ideas made the farming industry grow and grow and grow in the South!

Match the name of each food George Washington Carver improved with its picture.

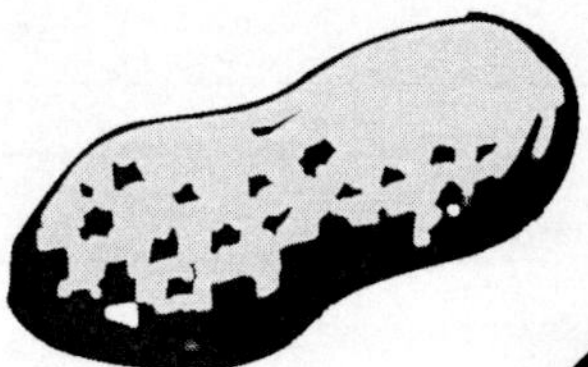

sweet potato

pecans

peanuts

Do some research to find the answers to the following questions.

1. **Carver created ice cream and sugar from:**
   a. wheat and barley
   b. peanut butter and jelly
   c. sweet potatoes and peanuts

2. **Carver was also known as:**
   a. an excellent speaker
   b. a famous politician
   c. a classical musician

3. **Congress honored Carver with:**
   a. the first federal monument dedicated to a Black person
   b. a government position
   c. a science award

4. **Carver became the first Black graduate of:**
   a. Howard University
   b. Harvard University
   c. Iowa State University

FAST FACT

More Stuff George Washington Carver Created From Plants... bleach, marble, shaving cream, dye, cheese, shampoo, instant coffee, shoe polish, mayonnaise, buttermilk, ink, chili sauce, paper, sugar, rubber, even steak sauce! But believe it or not... George did not discover peanut butter!

Answers: 1. c, 2. a, 3. a, 4. c

Word Factory

Let's brainstorm! Write as many words as you can from the letters in the phrase below.

"BLACK HISTORY!"

Black Cabinet Leaders!

The President of the United States appoints a "Cabinet" after winning an election. Members of the presidential Cabinet are asked to support and advise the president. Other people are also asked to help in specific positions. Many African Americans have served in Cabinet positions.

Unscramble the words to discover facts about each U.S. leader.

FACTS ABOUT OUR BLACK LEADERS

1. Colin Powell was appointed the first black U.S. Secretary of TTSAE ______________.
2. Eric Holder became the first black Attorney AGREENL ______________.
3. Colin Powell served in Persian FGLU ________ War as a Four-star General.
4. Condoleezza Rice was appointed the first black YRESCERTA ________________ of State.
5. Loretta Lynch became the first Black AFEELM Attorney General.
6. Condoleezza Rice trained as a competitive ice KTERSA ____________ and concert pianist.

Answers: 1. State, 2. General, 3. Gulf, 4. Secretary, 5. female, 6. skater

Where in the World Is Africa?

Africa is a continent made up of many countries. North America only has three countries! A hemisphere is one half of the Earth. The Equator divides the Earth into the Northern Hemisphere and the Southern Hemisphere. The Prime Meridian divides the Earth into the Eastern Hemisphere and the Western Hemisphere.

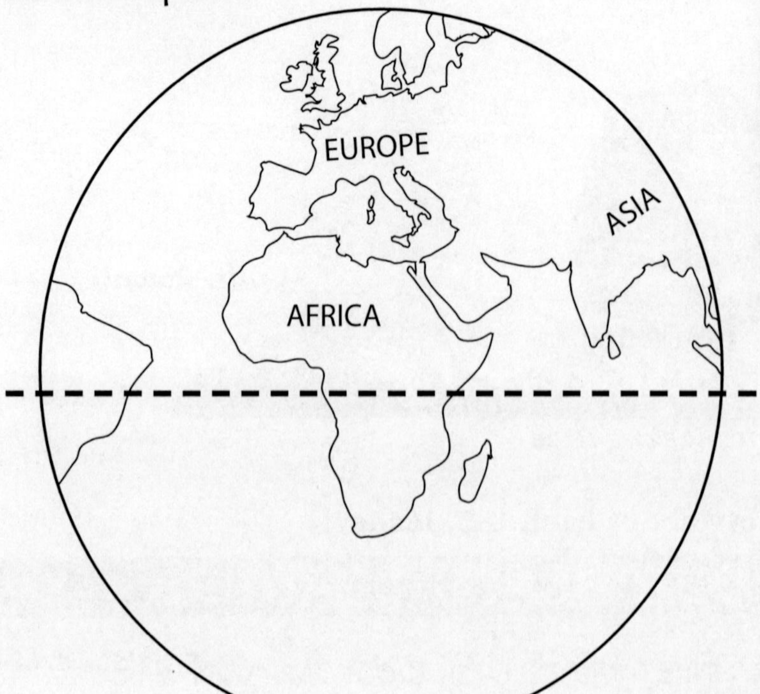

Label the Northern Hemisphere. Label the Southern Hemisphere. Write E on the equator. Is Africa in the NORTHERN HEMISPHERE or the SOUTHERN HEMISPHERE? Color Northern Africa red. Color Southern Africa orange.

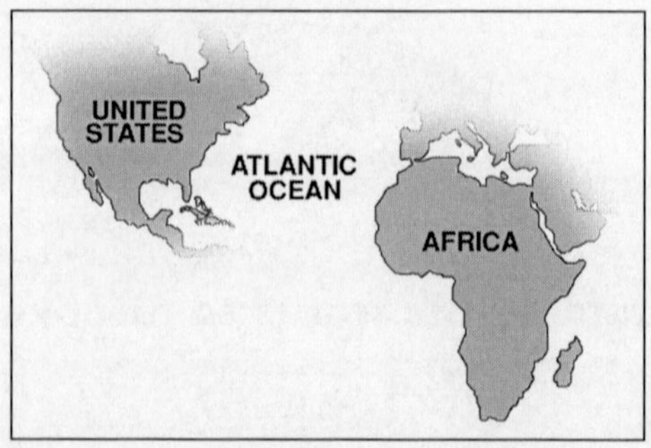

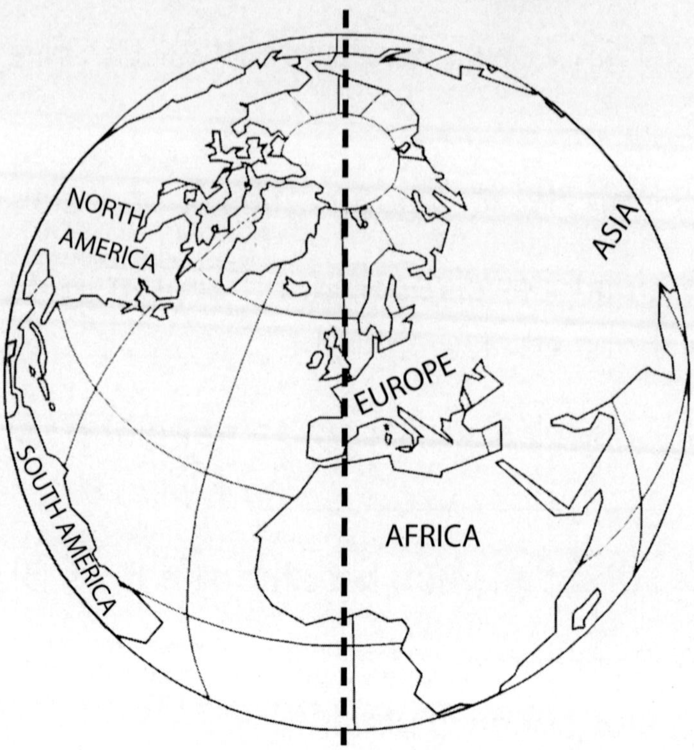

Label the Eastern Hemisphere. Label the Western Hemisphere. Write PM on the Prime Meridian. Is Africa in the EASTERN HEMISPHERE or WESTERN HEMISPHERE? Color Eastern Africa Green. Color Western Africa blue.

Answer: Africa lies in both hemispheres!

To Be or Not To Be?

African American poets introduce new thoughts and different ideas to our culture. Like the words of any other group of people, the Black perspective is unique! We can learn many things by reading what others have written. As readers, we must think carefully to decide whether or not we agree with what we read. Ask a teacher or parent to help you find poetry from an African American writer. Below are just a few examples of excellent Black poets.

Many Black poets share their feelings about the difficult trials of their people, like slavery and racism, within their work. Write an original poem about a problem that you have overcome or a difficulty that you have faced. Be sure to use lots of action verbs and colorful adjectives!

Phillis Wheatley was a famous poet. She was an enslaved woman who learned to read and write.

Famous Black Poets:

- Gwendolyn Brooks
- Maya Angelou
- Toni Morrison
- Alice Walker
- Langston Hughes
- Countee Cullen
- Phillis Wheatley

Underground Railroad Word Search

Thousands of enslaved people escaped to find freedom in the North. Some succeeded, and some were sent back to the South. Many enslaved people traveled along the Underground Railroad, a network of safe places where they could hide and friends who could help. Harriet Tubman, known as the "Moses" of her people, was a famous "conductor" who led more than 300 people to freedom.

Use the Word Bank to find the words in the word search below.

WORD SEARCH

Underground • fugitive • abolitionist • capture • Railroad • law
Harriet Tubman • freedom • miles • North • hide • swamp • reunion
capture • African • route • South • danger • slaveowner • family
equal • fear • escape

```
L A L H S I Q C U M S S N O R T H
A B O L I T I O N I S T O Q B V P
W R A Y A D S F D B E S I U Z E K
C V S L S R E H E L V P N F T O R
E W Z A F A M S R S I O U D E H O
T N K U R O X V G J T U E R C A T
S A R Q D F S C R A I L R O A D C
E C T E J N N A O U G D S U P H U
R I E S C A P E U Y U X M T T T D
O R O S E K I M N U F U G E U W N
F F A M I L Y A D A N G E R R E O
H A R R I E T T U B M A N S E I C
V E S L A L S R E N W O E V A L D
```

Amen!

The African Baptist Church, the first known Black church, was established in 1758. Today there are many kinds of Black churches in America, like the African Methodist Episcopal Church and the African Orthodox Church.

FAST FACT

Martin Luther King Jr., his father, and his grandfather all preached at Ebenezer Baptist Church in Atlanta, Georgia.

Color the church and Bible.

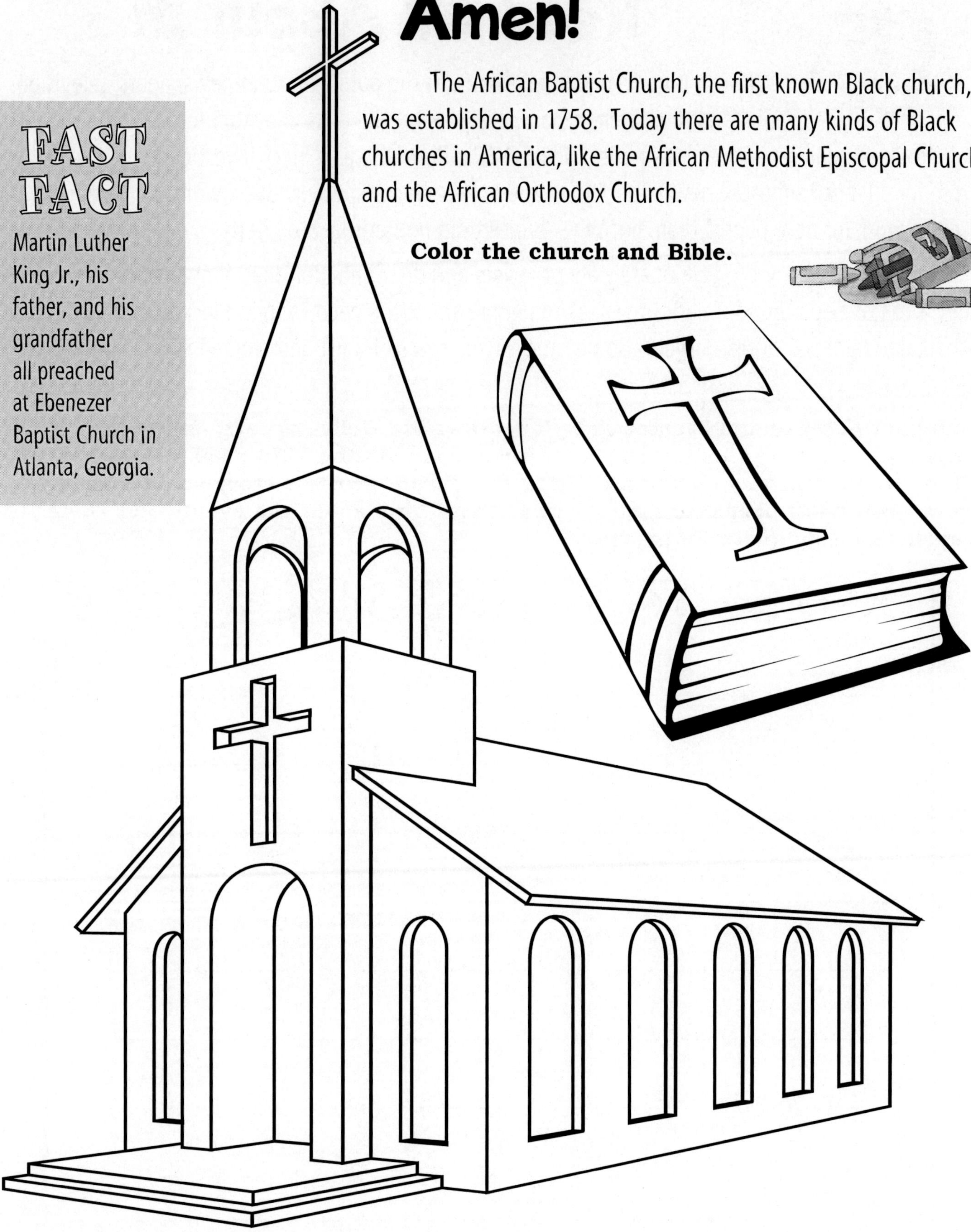

Read All About It!

African American journalists inform the public through newspapers, television, radio, and the internet. Journalists report the facts in a story format. They must be ready to investigate at a moment's notice! Ida B. Wells-Barnett was a Black investigative journalist who wrote for a Black Tennessee newspaper in the 1800s. Women (especially Black women) were not often hired to work for newspapers then, but Wells-Barnett did not let that stop her!

Wells-Barnett wrote passionately about racism and discrimination that happened in her state. Later, she traveled around America to speak to people about the need to treat Black people with more respect and fairness. Wells-Barnett also became a women's suffragist and worked to give women the right to vote.

Grab your notepad and become today's fearless Ida Wells-Barnett. Journalists, like Wells-Barnett, write their stories by using a basic outline. They ask who, what, where, when, and why questions. Using this format, write a story about a school event. Interview people to find out what they think about the event. Put their responses inside quotation marks.

Free States & Slave States

During the early centuries of American history, some states allowed slavery and some states did not. As of 1860, slave states included Alabama, Arkansas, Delaware, Florida, Georgia, Kentucky, Louisiana, Maryland, Mississippi, Missouri, North Carolina, South Carolina, Tennessee, Texas, and Virginia.

Free states included California, Connecticut, Illinois, Iowa, Indiana, Maine, Massachusetts, Michigan, Minnesota, New Hampshire, New Jersey, New York, Ohio, Oregon, Pennsylvania, Rhode Island, Vermont, and Wisconsin. Enslaved people used different routes to escape to freedom in the free Northern states, Canada, Mexico, or even the Caribbean.

Color the free states blue. Color the slave states red.
Color the other states green.

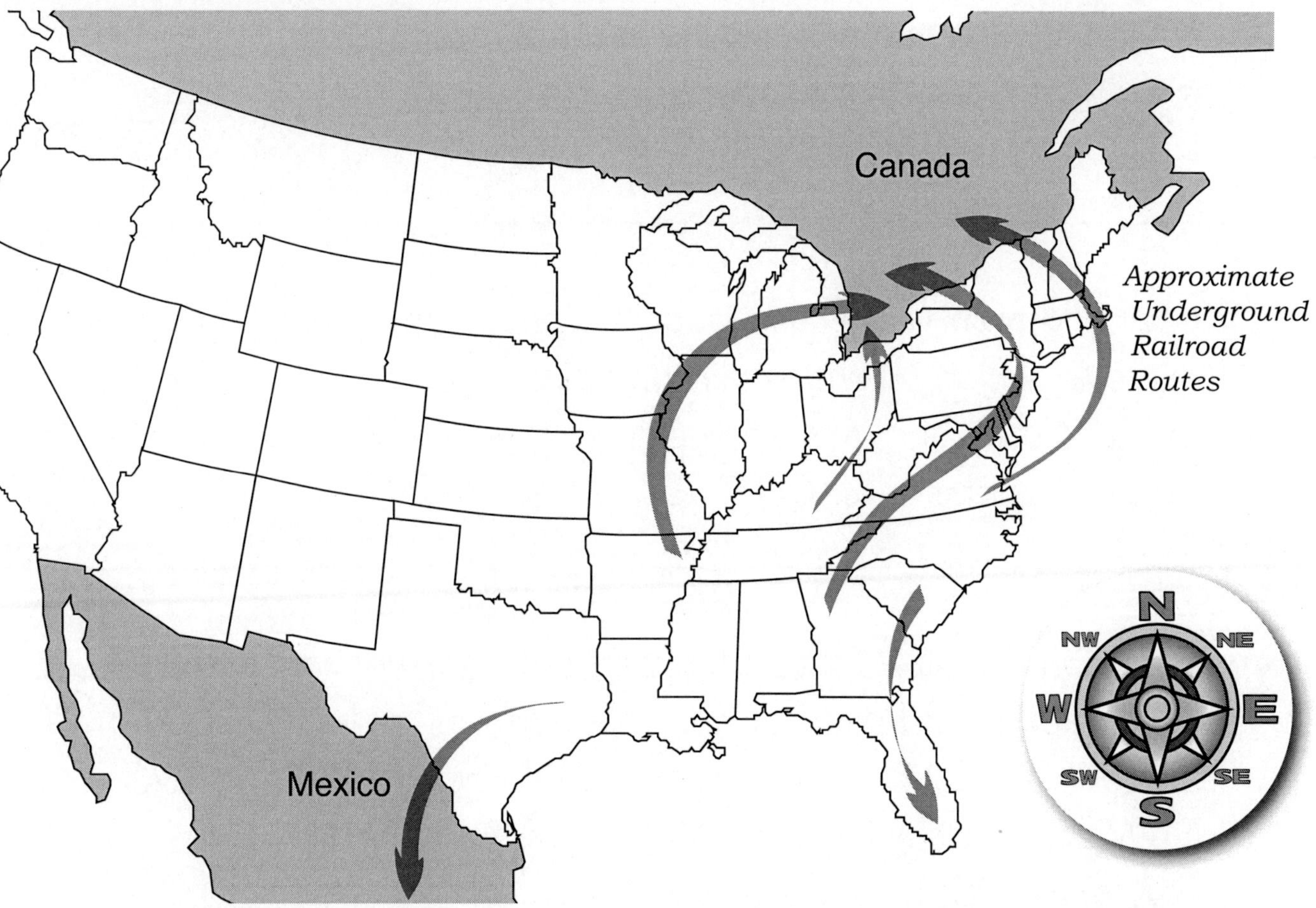

FAST FACT

Harriet Tubman helped more than 300 enslaved people escape!

Hit That Note!

Complete the activities to learn about these famous African American performers!

1. Starting with the letter C, cross out every other letter to spell the nickname of famous blues musician W.C. Handy, who was born in 1873.
CFKARTTHYENRBOVFGTFHDEEBWLTUYEUSI
____

2. Starting with the letter B, cross out every other letter to find out who taught the legendary Nat King Cole to play the piano at age 4.
BHTIGSHMIOOTPHSEWRV
____

3. Starting with the letter M, cross out every other letter to discover which talented blind musician sang *Georgia on My Mind*, now the official state song of Georgia.
MRTAEYVCBHNAMROLPESSD
____

4. Starting with the letter J, cross out every other letter to see where actor and singer Paul Robeson was educated.
JRKULTOGPEWRTSYUGNHINVMERRTSGIYTHYNAJNKDG
CTOVLFURMEBWIFAGUHNHIJVKELRTSGIYTHYULJAIWI
SOCWHSODOFLG ____
____
____

Answers: 1. Father of the Blues, 2. his mother, 3. Ray Charles, 4. Rutgers University and Columbia University Law School

It's Money in the Bank!

Did you know that Maggie Lena Walker became the first female bank president in 1903? She was a very famous businesswoman in her time. She headed the St. Luke Penny Savings Bank. It was founded by the Grand United Order of St. Luke, a group of people who taught African Americans how to save money and support each other in business!

Let's say that you're in college. Over the summer, you worked really hard as an intern with the National Association for the Advancement of Colored People (NAACP) bureau in Washington, D.C. You earned a lot of experience and a decent amount of money... $500 to be exact! How much will you save? How much will you spend? Solve the math problems below to find out how your earnings might be spent.

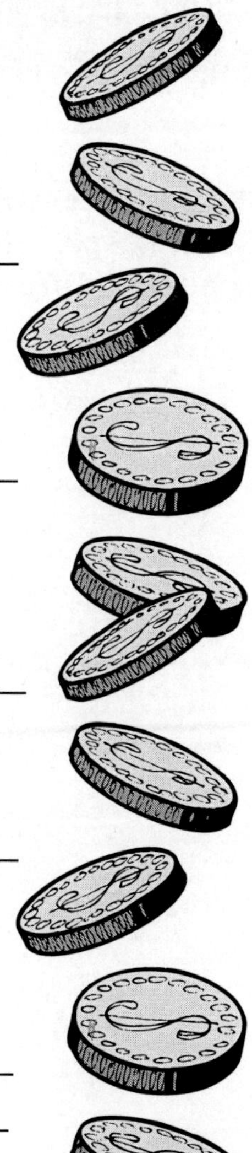

TOTAL EARNED: $500.00

I will pay back my Mom this much (A) for money I borrowed when I first started working. Thanks, Mom! — A. $20.00

subtract A from $500 = (B) — B. ____________

I will give my little brother this much money (C) for helping me with my chores when I had to work late: — C. $10.00

subtract C from B = (D) — D. ____________

I will spend this much (E) on a special treat for myself: — E. $25.00

subtract E from D = (F) — F. ____________

I will save this much (G) for college: — G. $300.00

subtract G from F = (H) — H. ____________

I will save this much (I) in a savings account to buy clothes: — I. $100.00

subtract I from H = (J) — J. ____________

TOTAL STILL AVAILABLE (use answer J) ____________

TOTAL SPENT (add A, C, and E) ____________

TOTAL SAVED (add G and I) ____________

Answers: B. $480, D. $470, F. $445, H. $145, J. $45, Total still available: $45, Total spent: $55, Total saved: $400

Civil Rights Movement

African Americans suffered from racial prejudice and discrimination long after the Civil War. Though they were made free citizens, they did not enjoy the same rights, privileges, or freedoms as the rest of America for decades. Some state laws kept Black Americans from voting, keeping weapons, running for political office, or working in certain jobs. Their schools, restaurants, neighborhoods, churches, even drinking fountains were all separate.

Finally, some people decided to try to end the discrimination. Dr. Martin Luther King Jr., a Black minister, worked hard to get equal rights. He spoke for the Black community, and he fought for equality for all people. He wanted people to work together for the common good of America. He encouraged people to help protest unfair laws through peaceful means without violence. Other civil rights heroes, like Rosa Parks and Thurgood Marshall, also helped bring about lasting change!

Follow the directions to make an Origami Peace Dove! Use the pictures to guide your steps. Keep the dove to remind yourself not to discriminate against people who are different than you. Or give the dove to someone else as a gift of peace!

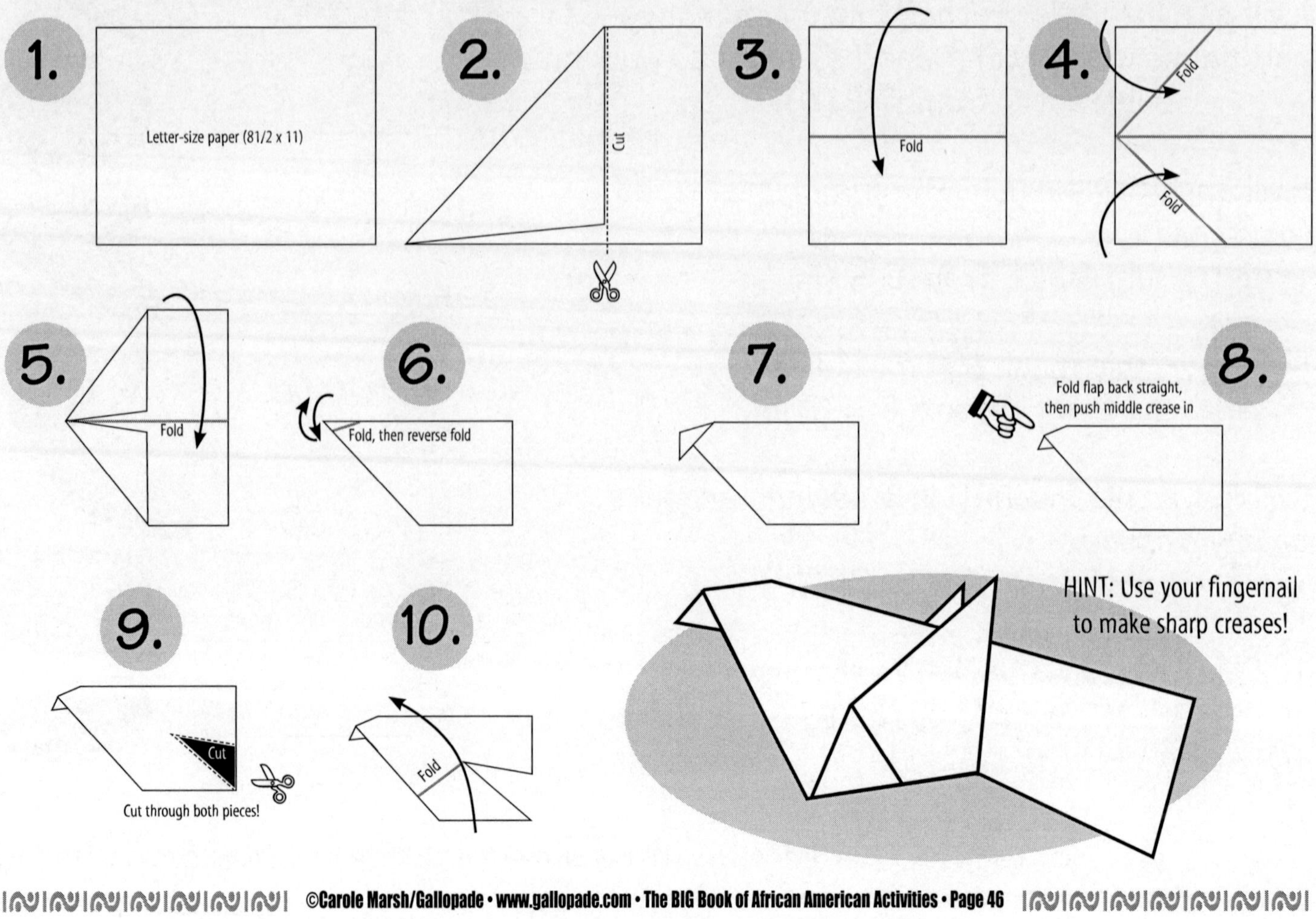

"Follow The Drinking Gourd"

Enslaved people often communicated messages to each other through song. This famous song provides direction to enslaved people who wished to escape on the Underground Railroad. What do you think these clues mean?

Write your response below.

When the sun comes back and the first quail calls,
Follow the Drinking Gourd.
For the old man is waiting for to carry you to freedom,
If you follow the Drinking Gourd.
The riverbank makes a very good road,
The dead trees show you the way,
Left foot, peg foot, traveling on
Follow the Drinking Gourd.
The river ends between two hills.
Follow the Drinking Gourd.
There's another river on the other side.
Follow the Drinking Gourd.
Where the great big river meets the little river,
Follow the Drinking Gourd.
For the old man is awaiting to carry you to freedom.
If you follow the Drinking Gourd.

NAACP Award

The National Association for the Advancement of Colored People (NAACP) is America's oldest and largest civil rights organization. In 1915, the group began awarding Spingarn Medals to African Americans who had made great achievements.

Color the Spingarn Medal.

Spingarn Medal Recipients:

- L. Douglas Wilder
- Percy E. Sutton
- Tom Bradley
- Lena Horne
- General Colin Powell
- Barbara Jordan
- Maya Angelou
- Dr. John Hope Franklin
- Judge A. Leon Higginbotham
- Carl Rowan
- Myrlie Evers-Williams

Black Firsts in the U.S. Coast Guard!

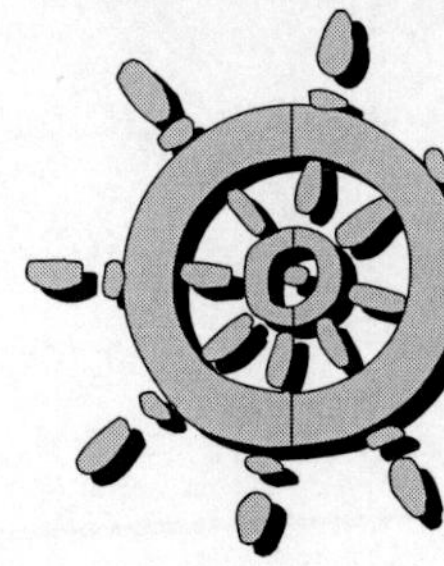

The U.S. Coast Guard was created in 1790. It used to be called the Revenue Marine. The U.S. Coast Guard is the smallest branch in the armed forces, but it is older than the U.S. Navy! African Americans have worked on ships since the early 1800s. However, they were not paid until 1831. Black seamen and seawomen have accomplished a great number of "firsts" in the U.S. Coast Guard!

Solve the math problems below to discover the year of some historical "firsts" for Black servicepeople in the U.S. Coast Guard.

1. The Treasury Department allows free people of color to be employed on board cutters (boats) as part of the crew.

   6-5 = _____ 4+4 = _____ 5-2 = _____ 9-8 = _____

2. First Lieutenant Michael Healy is the first African-American to command a U.S. military vessel.

   0+1 = _____ 8+0 = _____ 4+3 = _____ 7x1 = _____

3. Richard Etheridge was the first African-American keeper of a U.S. Life-Saving Station, and he commanded the only all African-American crew in the U.S.

   1x1 = _____ 3+5 = _____ 8x1 = _____ 8x0 = _____

4. Erroll Brown becomes the first African-American admiral in the Coast Guard.

   3-2 = _____ 3+3+3 = _____ 4+5 = _____ 4+4 = _____

5. The cutter (boat) Sea Cloud becomes the first U.S. military vessel to sail with a fully racially integrated crew.

   8-7 = _____ 8+1 = _____ 8-4 = _____ 7-4 = _____

6. President Harry Truman orders the integration of the armed forces of the United States. By this time the Coast Guard had already opened up all of its ranks to all qualified persons regardless of race.

   4-3 = _____ 7+2 = _____ 2x2 = _____ 5+3 = _____

Answers: 1. 1831, 2. 1877, 3. 1880, 4. 1998, 5. 1943, 6. 1948

Attention, Class!

Enslaved people were not allowed to read or write. It was illegal to teach Black children. But many enslaved people learned in secret. Even a few white plantation owners broke the laws to teach those they enslaved because they wanted them to do tasks involving reading or writing skills.

Black educators had to teach Black boys and girls how to succeed in a world that didn't want them to succeed. Education reformer Booker T. Washington was a world renowned famous Black educator at the Tuskegee Institute (pronounced tusk-E-gee) in the late 1800s. He emphasized education as the best way to improve the way Black people were treated.

Mary McLeod Bethune received an education funded by a kindly Quaker teacher. Bethune wanted other poor Black children to have an opportunity to learn as she did. Starting with $1.50 in her pocket, Bethune founded Bethune-Cookman College in the early 1900s. She sold sweet potato pies and wrote letters to fund the school. Later Bethune won a Spingarn Medal for her achievements.

Make each false statement true. Cross out the false word and write the correct word in the blank.

1. Booker T. Washington worked as a gardener. ____________

2. Enslaved people were not allowed to read or sew. ____________

3. Black plantation owners sometimes taught their slaves illegally. ____________

4. Mary McLeod Bethune sold apple pies to fund her college. ____________

5. Booker T. Washington taught at the Turtle Institute. ____________

6. Teaching enslaved Black children was allowed. ____________

Answers: 1. False – educator, 2. False – write, 3. True, 4. False – sweet potato, 5. False – Tuskegee, 6. False – not allowed

Black History in the Zone!

Black history takes place all over America, in every state and in every time zone. The continental U.S. is divided into four time zones. There is a one-hour time difference between each zone. The earth's rotation makes the sun look like it travels from east to west, but the sun doesn't move from its fixed position!

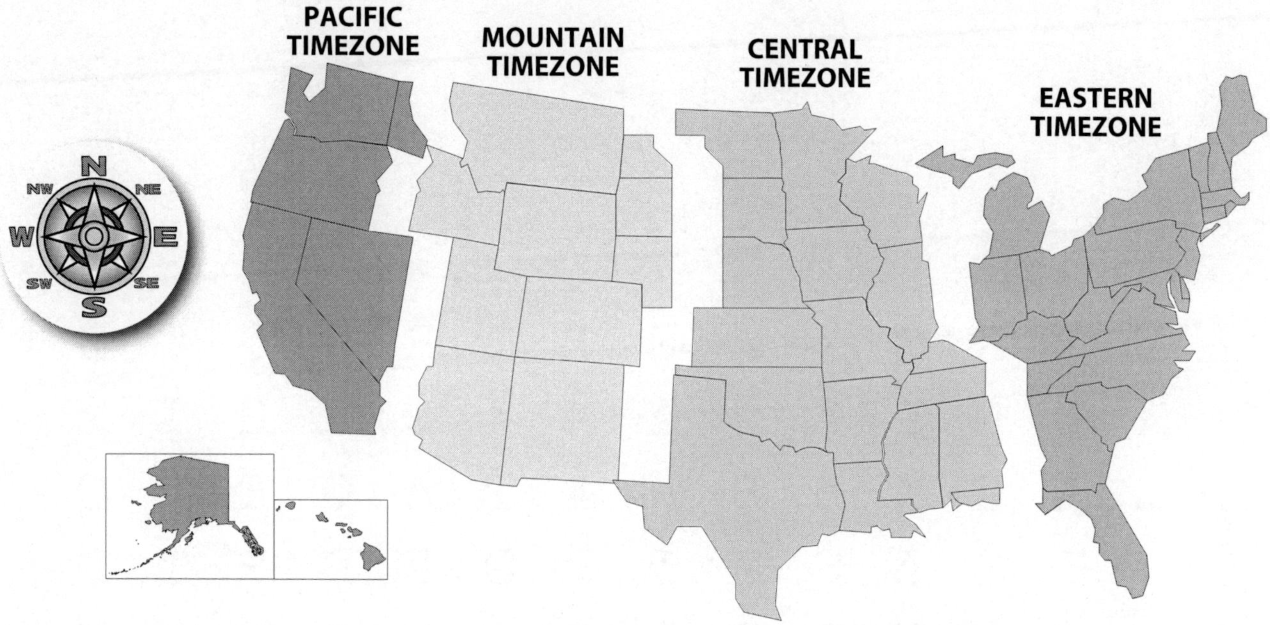

Using the time zones on the map above, answer the following questions. Then label the states found in each question.

1. In 1811, the largest rebellion of enslaved people in U.S. history took place in New Orleans, Louisiana. In what time zone did the rebellion occur? ____________________

2. In 1905, nine Black students formed the first Black fraternity, Alpha Phi Alpha, at Cornell University in New York. In what time zone did this event occur? ____________________

3. In 1895, Henry Flipper became the first Black editor of a white newspaper, the *Nogales Sunday Herald*, in Nogales, Arizona. In which time zone did this event occur? ____________________

4. William Leidesdorff operated the world's first steamboat in San Francisco, California in 1847. In what time zone did this occur? ____________________

5. Barbara Jordan was elected to the U.S. House of Representatives in 1972. This victory made her the first Black Texan in the U.S. Congress. In what time zone did this event occur?

____

Answers: 1. Central, 2. Eastern, 3. Mountain, 4. Pacific, 5. Central

The Great African American Word Search!

Studying Black heritage can make lots of words come to mind. Some words might be new, but you have learned most of these hidden words just by completing activities in this book!

Circle the words in the Word Search below.
You may have to look in ALL different directions!

WORD SEARCH

Africa • black heritage • boycott • civil rights
education • emancipation • freedom • history
invent • medal • MLK • NAACP • pride
science • senator • Spingarn • writer

J X T K Q I R E T I R W G C Z
U K T N P A U A N K R K H I M
B L A C K H E R I T A G E V O
E J T S A S M T P O P D R I D
V M F T E A I L C O U K M L E
Z K A U O N B O A C W U B R E
Y D Z N V C A Q A Y Y Z F I R
B O T E C E Y T N R H T A G F
A A N T D I I O O W L J Z H Y
F T D I D O P T B R N A M T T
R E R E N N S A S Z S Z D S I
I P G Q I I B G T G M L K E Y
C J D M H V C S C I E N C E M
A X P K Y Z R L H W O N O D C
W R K N R A G N I P S N L R A

Black Magazine Publishing

His media empire grew to include several popular magazines focused on the interests of African Americans. Black publisher John Harold Johnson borrowed $500 to start the Johnson Publishing Company in 1942. His media empire grew to include several popular magazines focused on the interests of African Americans.

Help John Harold Johnson publish his magazine.
Number each box to put the steps of the publishing process in logical order.

Writers research and write articles.

Editors correct mistakes in the articles.

Printing press prints magazines onto paper.

Trucks deliver magazines to stores.

Sales representatives sell magazine ads.

Graphic artists lay out photographs.

Readers love their magazines!

Answers: 1, 3, 5, 6, 4, 2, 7

Black Pioneers Head West!

During the 1800s, many settlers traveled West in caravans of covered wagons. Black pioneers rode down those dusty paths as well, looking for a new way of life. Black pioneer children didn't have video games or soccer balls to play with so they got creative!

Follow the direction below to make a corn husk doll!

YOU WILL NEED:

- corn husks (or strips of cloth)
- string
- scissors

1. Select a long piece of corn husk and fold it in half. Tie a string about one inch (2.54 centimeters) down from the fold to make the doll's head.

2. Roll a husk and put it between the layers of the tied husk, next to the string. Tie another string around the longer husk, just below the rolled husk. Now your doll has arms! Tie short pieces of string at the ends of the rolled husk to make the doll's hands.

3. Make your doll's waist by tying another string around the longer husk.

4. If you want your doll to have legs, cut the longer husk up the middle. Tie the two halves at the bottom to make feet.

5. Add eyes and a nose to your doll with a marker. You could use corn silk for the doll's hair.

Now you can make a whole family of dolls!

Equality is...

Americans want equality in their country. Everyone should be treated equally without discrimination. What does equality mean to you?

Using each letter of the word "equality," write a word or phrase that describes equality.

E is for EVERYONE!

Q is for ______________________________

U is for ______________________________

A is for ______________________________

L is for ______________________________

I is for ______________________________

T is for ______________________________

Y is for ______________________________

African American Trivia

Unscramble the words to discover amazing African American trivia!

WORD BANK

heart rookie Grammy Honor poet People Kansas

1. Twenty-two Black soldiers won the Medal of NOOHR __________ while serving in the Union Army during the Civil War!

2. The initials NAACP stand for National Association for the Advancement of Colored PPLEOE __________.

3. Wilt Chamberlain, NBA OORKEI __________ of the Year in 1960, was the leading team scorer for 7 years in a row.

4. Gwendolyn Brooks, noted Black TEPO __________, was the first African American to win a Pulitzer Prize.

5. Stevie Wonder captured 3 out of 4 of the MYMARG __________ Awards for Male Pop Vocalist from 1973 through 1976.

6. Dr. Daniel Hale Williams performed the first open THARE __________ operation and founded Chicago's first Black hospital, Provident.

7. The famous lawsuit Brown vs. Board of Education, which started the desegregation of American schools, took place in Topeka, SSNAKA __________.

Answers: 1. Honor; 2. People; 3. Rookie; 4. poet; 5. Grammy; 6. heart; 7. Kansas

Supreme Court Bubblegram!

The U.S. Supreme Court is the highest court in America. Only the most important cases are heard there by the Chief Justice and the eight Associate Justices. Only the president can nominate justices.

Thurgood Marshall was one of the most famous Supreme Court Justices in U.S. history. His influence on the court helped make many changes in civil rights legislation, including school desegregation.

Another famous justice is African American Clarence Thomas. He was nominated In 1990 by President George H. Bush. After the Senate approved his nomination, Clarence took his seat on October 23, 1991.

Fill in the bubblegram by using the clues below.
Some letters are already filled in for you.

1. Black Associate Justice nominated by George Bush
2. The only person who can nominate justices for the Supreme Court
3. Thurgood Marshall helped __________ American schools
4. The number of Associate Justices on the Supreme Court
5. Black justice who was also a civil rights hero
6. The highest court in America

1. _ _ A _ _ _ _ _ _ H _ _ _ (_)
2. _ _ E _ _ _ _ (_) _
3. D _ _ _ _ G _ _ _ (_) _
4. (_) _ _ _ T
5. _ _ _ _ G _ _ _ (_) _ _ _ _ _ L
6. S _ _ _ _ _ _ _ _ U _ (_)

Unscramble the "bubble" letters to find out the mystery answer!

Mystery Question: Who approves the president's nominations for a justice?
Hint: You'll find them on Capitol Hill in Washington, D.C.!
Mystery Word: ___ ___ ___ ___ ___ ___

Answers: 1. Clarence Thomas; 2. president; 3. desegregate; 4. eight; 5. Thurgood Marshall; 6. Supreme Court **Mystery Answer:** Senate

The *Amistad*

In 1839, a ship called the *Amistad* was discovered in the Long Island Sound in Connecticut. It was filled with enslaved Africans who had taken control of the ship. Connecticut authorities arrested the Africans and put them in jail. Then, the Spanish and Cuban governments sued the United States demanding the return of the formerly enslaved people to them.

A lawyer named Roger Sherman Baldwin asked the Connecticut court to free the Africans. He won the case, but it was appealed all the way to the U.S. Supreme Court. John Quincy Adams allowed the judgment to stand. The 35 Black men, women, and children sailed back to their homeland!

Use information from the story to complete the crossword below.

1. The enslaved ________________ took over a ship from their enslavers. (ACROSS)

2. This ship they took over was named the ________________. (DOWN)

3. ________________ Sherman Baldwin was a lawyer who tried to free the enslaved people. (DOWN)

4. The Spanish and Cuban governments demanded the ________________ of the formerly enslaved people to them. (ACROSS)

5. The case was ________________ to the Supreme Court. (DOWN)

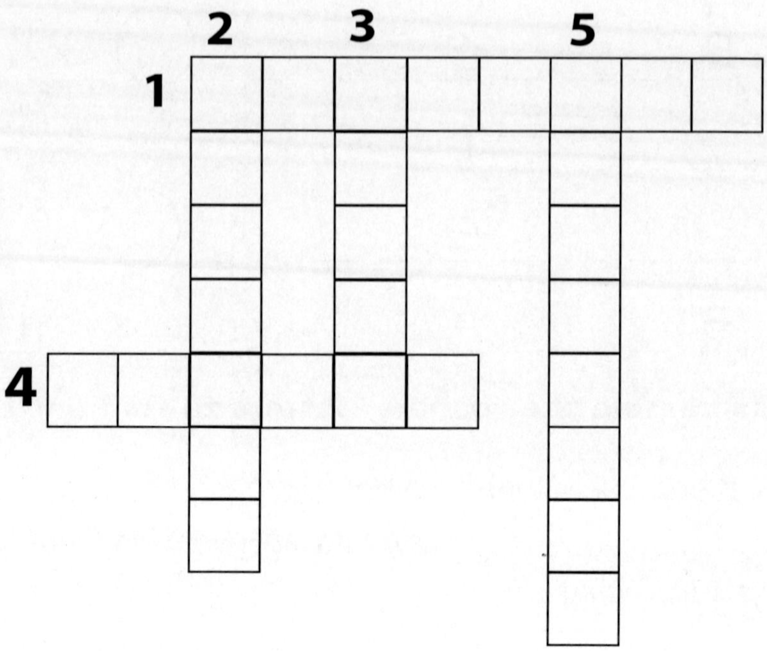

Answers: 1 Africans, 2 Amistad, 3 Roger, 4 return, 5 appealed

King Had a Dream

In 1963, Dr. Martin Luther King Jr. delivered a famous speech in Washington, D.C. He told many people about his special dream. Dr. King dreamed of a world in which Black boys and girls could play with white boys and girls peacefully. This speech was presented on the steps of the Lincoln Memorial during the March on Washington. The march was a movement where thousands of people gathered at the nation's capital to protest inequality.

Color the Lincoln Memorial.

The Harlem Renaissance!

Great creativity and original thought poured out of New York City between 1919 and 1937. This era was known as the "Harlem Renaissance." During this time, Black artists celebrated their pride and love for their roots and heritage.

Gifted African American writers produced fiction, drama, poetry, and essays. Black musicians also heavily influenced several music forms such as jazz and blues. Black artists became more well known. African American theater boomed with the popular 1921 Broadway musical *Shuffle Along*, performed by an all-Black cast in New York City.

Study the quote from W.E.B. Du Bois (pronounced doo-b`wah). What is the author trying to say to the reader? Write your response below.

"Children learn more from what you are than what you teach."

Great Black Authors in History: Toni Morrison, Alice Walker, Eldridge Cleaver, Booker T. Washington, Frederick Douglass, W.E.B. Du Bois, Olaudah Equiano, James Meredith, and Toni Cade Bambara

Up, Up and Away!

During World War II, many Black men left homes in farms, towns, and cities across America to volunteer as Tuskegee Airmen. They were the first Black military airmen to serve in the United States armed forces. After graduating from air training, many Tuskegee Airmen became pilots, navigators, or bombardiers. Several airmen became officers, and many served in supporting ground positions.

The Tuskegee Airmen faced doubt, war, and racial discrimination. But they overcame them all!

Follow the directions to build a paper airplane! Use the pictures to help guide your steps. Fold an 8 1/2 x 11" sheet of paper in half lengthwise. Next, fold down the corners as shown. Then fold each side down to the center again, and then again as shown in the picture. Decorate your plane to celebrate African American achievements. Be creative!

Charles "Chief" Anderson, a famous Black pilot, trained Tuskegee Airmen and once took Eleanor Roosevelt up for a ride!

1 2

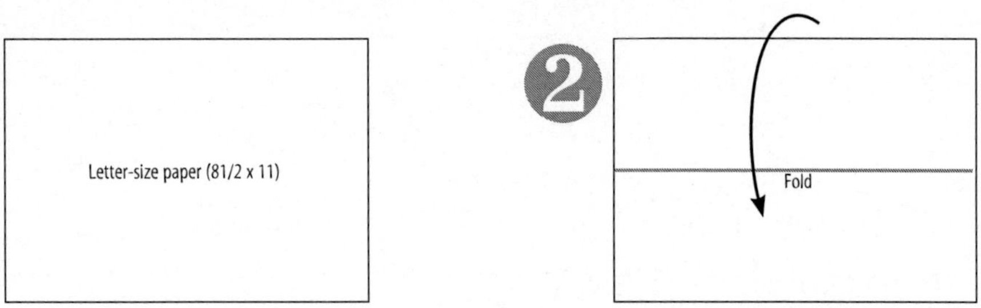

3 4 5

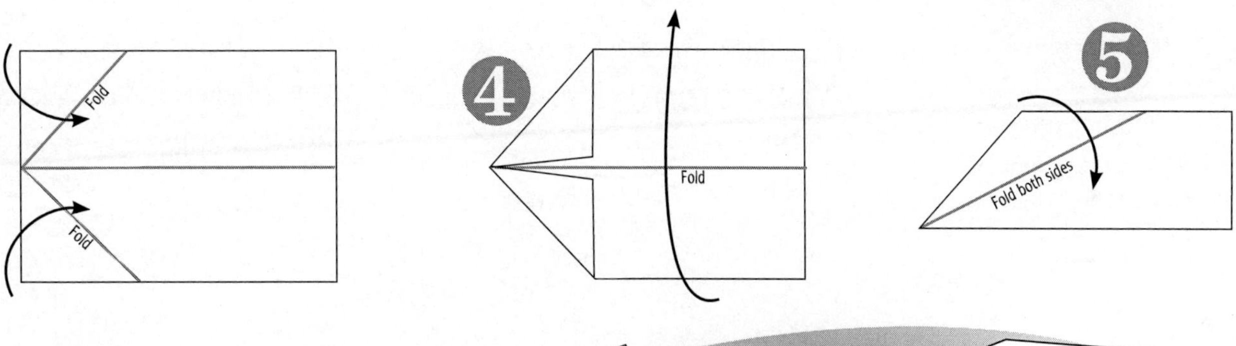

6

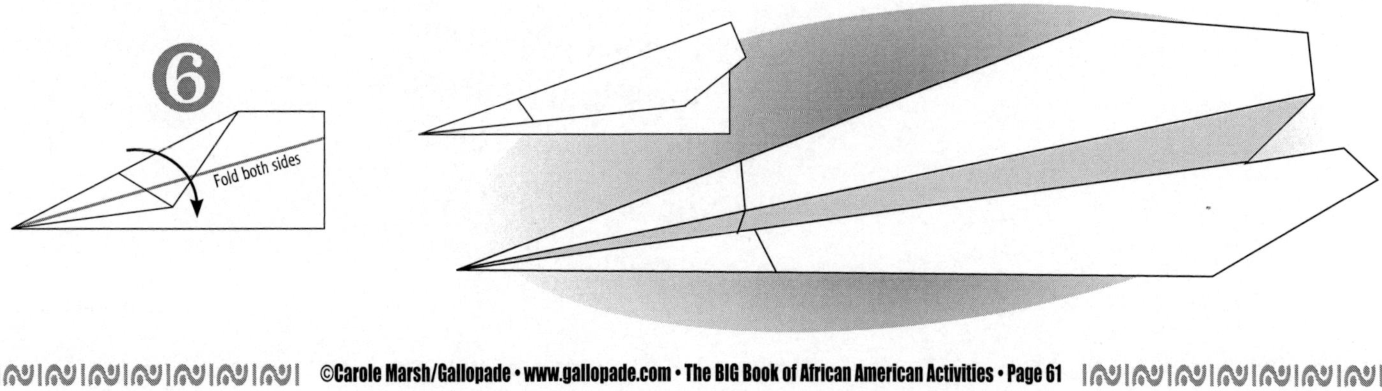

Map to the Stars

People escaping slavery often used star constellations in the sky to help them find the right path to freedom. Constellations are groups of stars that can represent images. A popular guidance constellation was the Drinking Gourd. Others included the Big and Little Dippers.

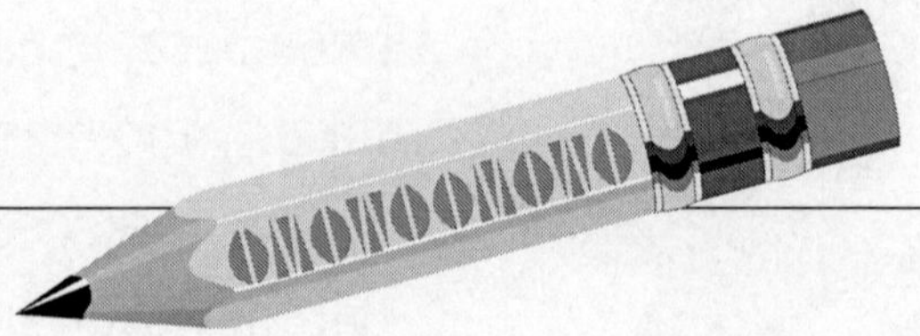

Complete the dot-to-dot of the constellations.

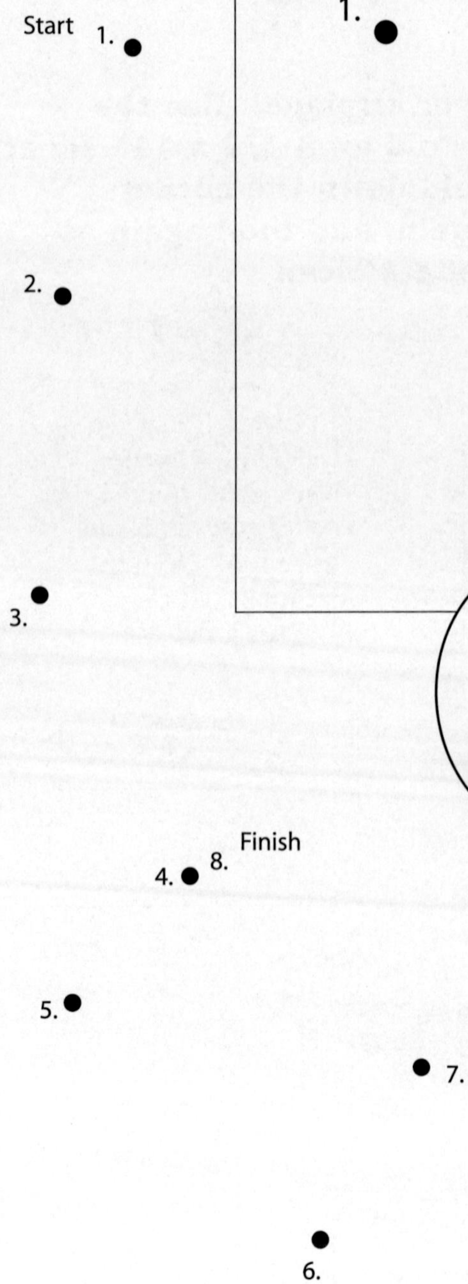

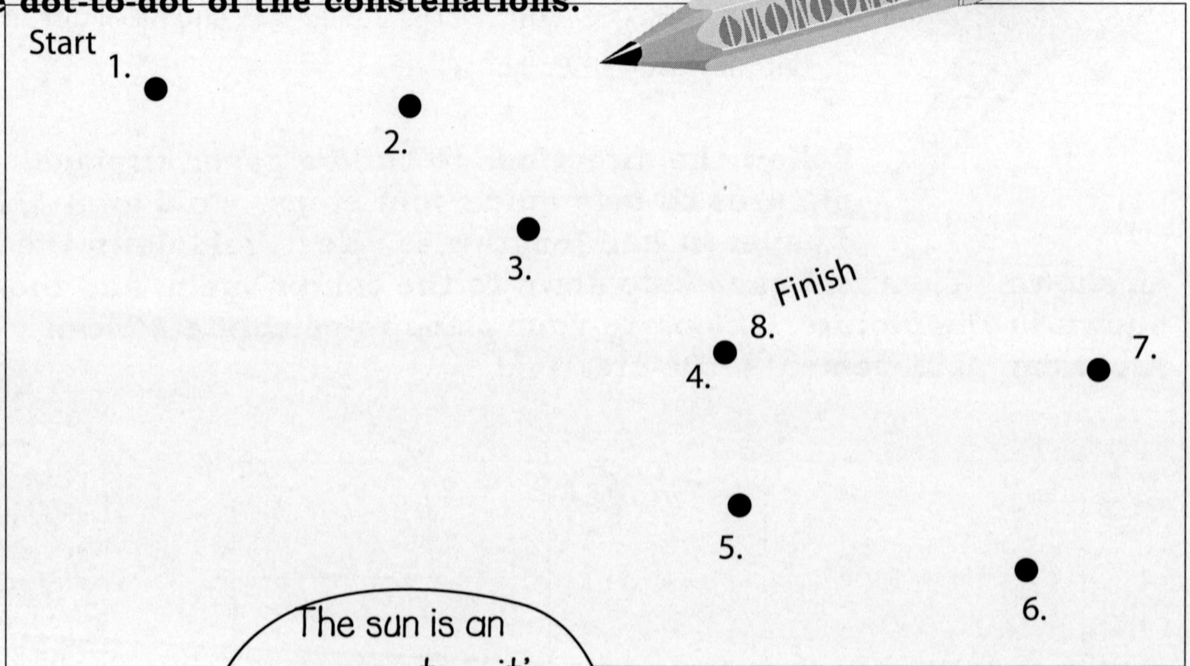

The sun is an average star–it's about 864,972 miles (1,392,000 kilometers) across!

There are 88 constellations! Wow! That's a lot of stars!

The handle on the Big Dipper curves downward and the handle on the Little Dipper curves upward.

Let's Sell Something New!

African Americans have invented many new products for many years. One innovative African American businesswoman is Sarah Breedlove McWilliams Walker. People called her Madame C.J. Walker. She was born enslaved and overcame difficult obstacles to become free. Walker invented an original treatment to straighten hair. She worked very hard to make her business grow. Walker's small business turned into a million-dollar enterprise... all from one simple idea.

Think about a product that you might like to make, such as a special family cookie recipe or a new toy. It could even be a new color for a crayon! Whatever you decide, it should be something that you think is fantastic enough for people to want to buy! Answer the following questions about your "new" product in the spaces below on the assembly line.

WHAT IS YOUR PRODUCT?

____

____

MARKETING:
Who will buy your product?

____

____

PRODUCTION:
How will your product be made?

____

____

____

FINANCE:
What will your product cost?

____

____

____

ADVERTISING:
How will people find out about your product?

____

____

____

Black Pioneer Maze

Jean Baptiste Point Du Sable is one of America's greatest pioneers! He was born in Haiti in 1745 to an enslaved mother and pirate father. During a trip to America, a hurricane destroyed his boat and Jean Baptiste found himself on the shores of New Orleans. He traveled up the Mississippi River until he reached St. Louis. Then Jean Baptiste moved to a lonely prairie region. He built a small settlement and trading post for traveling explorers, hunters, trappers, settlers, and missionaries. Jean Baptiste's settlement GREW and GREW and GREW until it became the present-day city of Chicago, Illinois!

Help Jean Baptiste survive the whirling hurricane and land safely on American shores.

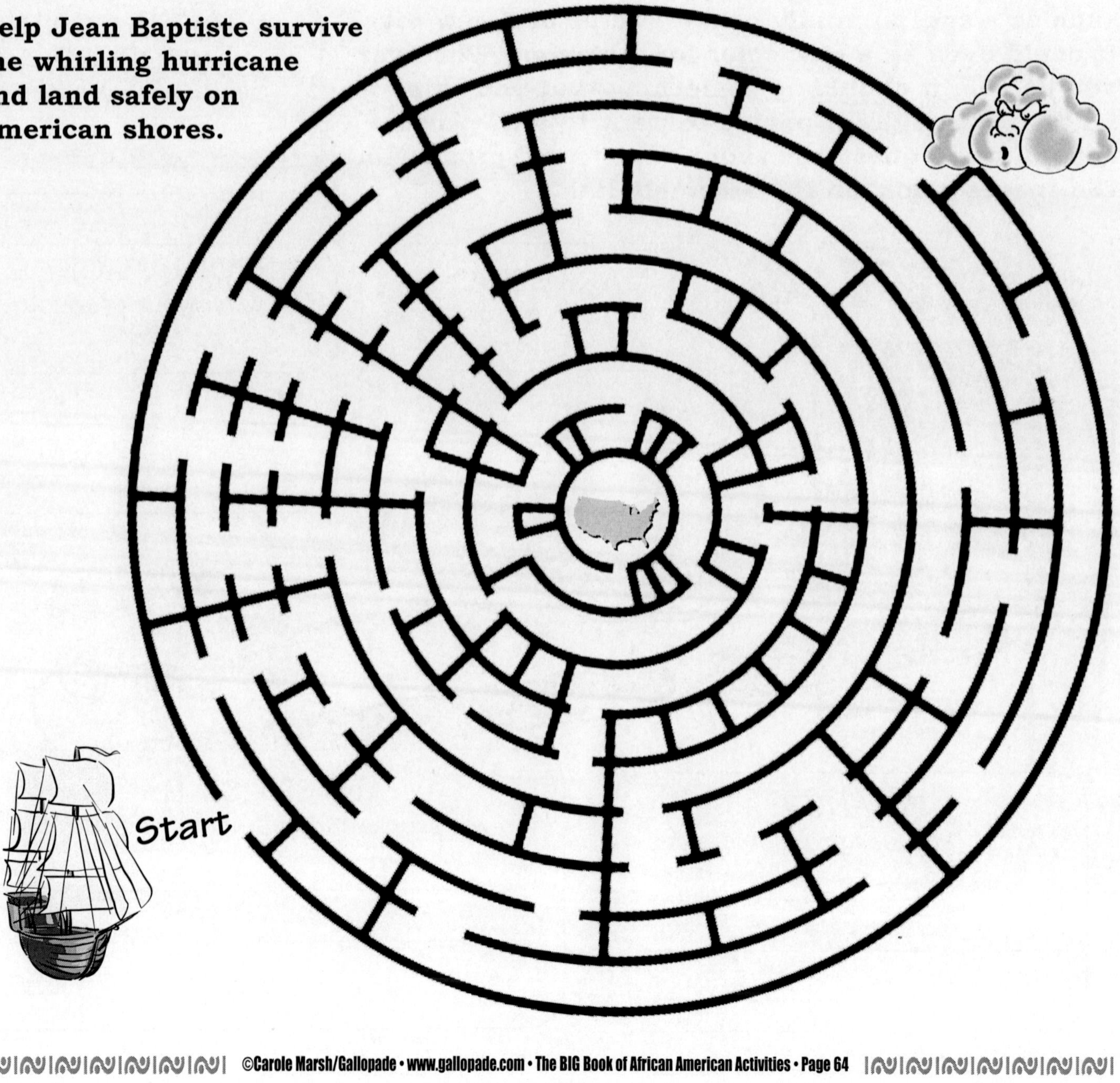

Virtual NAACP

The National Association for the Advancement of Colored People (NAACP) is the oldest civil rights organization in the United States. A group of young activists formed the NAACP in 1909 to help improve the lives of Black people. The NAACP leads civil right rallies and protests, maintains a Youth Council, and publishes *Crisis* magazine. The non-profit also organizes voters to register for public elections, stays involved with public policy issues to enact change in U.S. government legislation, and fights discrimination by bringing legal cases to courts.

Imagine that the NAACP has asked you to design a new web page for them. Design a creative web page that tells people all about the NAACP!

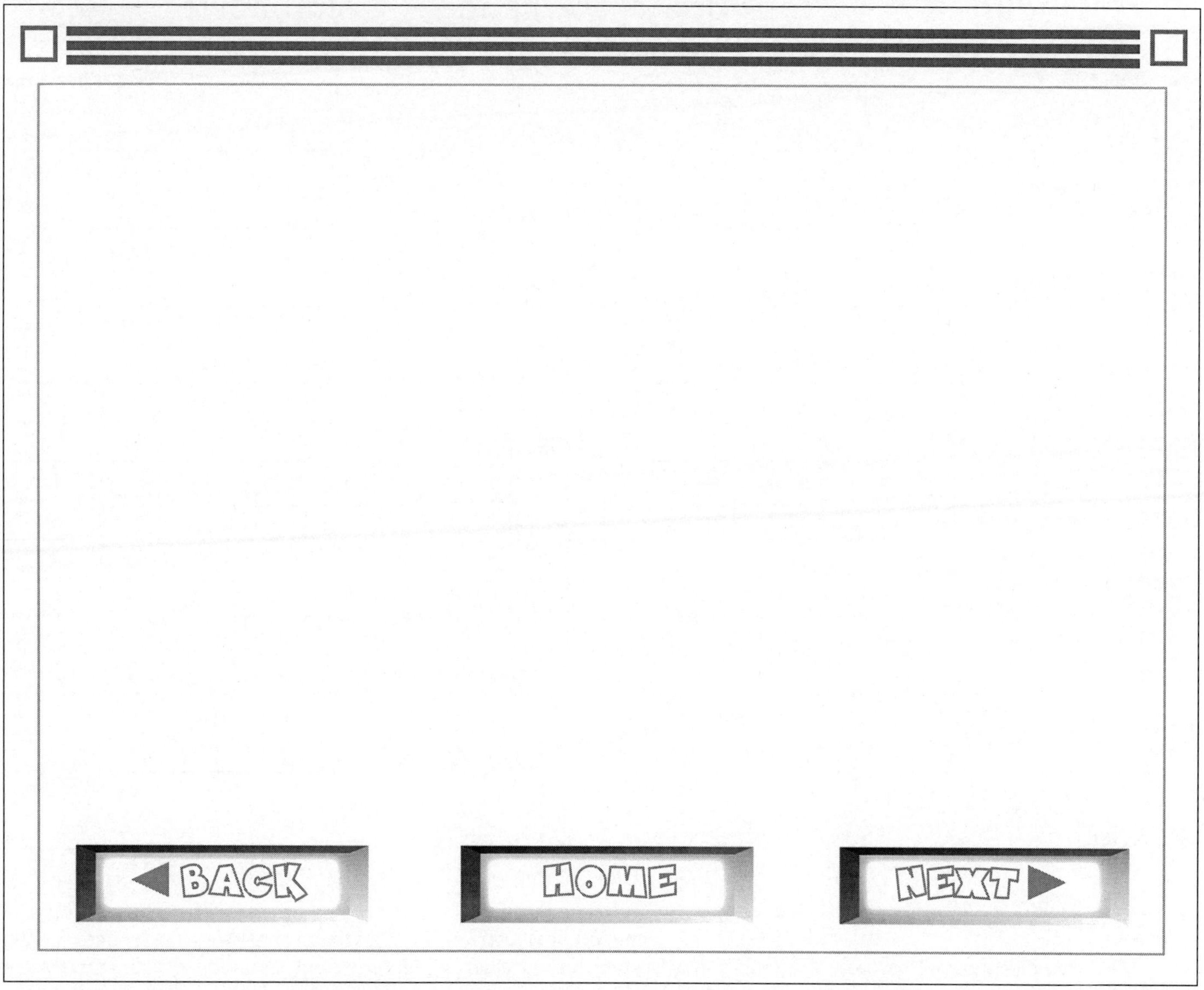

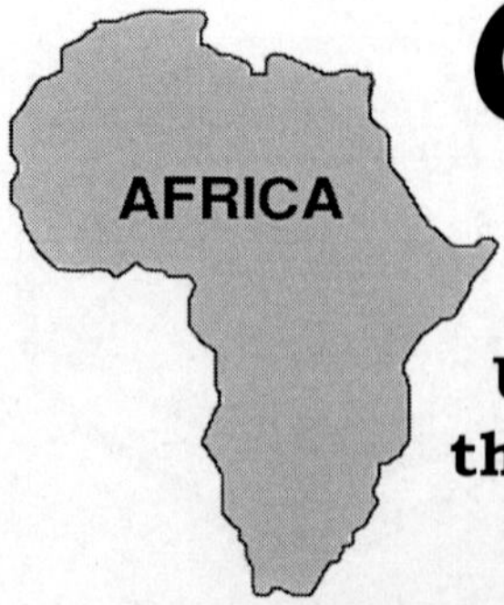

Countries of Africa Jumble

There are more than 50 countries on the continent of Africa.

Unscramble the names of some of these African countries. Use the Word Bank for help.

WORD BANK

Algeria	Chad	Egypt	Ethiopia
Ghana	Angola	Kenya	Liberia
Madagascar	Mali	Morocco	Nigeria
Rwanda	Senegal	Somalia	South Africa
Sudan	Tanzania	Uganda	Zimbabwe

DHAC	________________	NESALEG	________________
ALERIBI	________________	ERNIGIA	________________
STHOU AARIFC	________ ________	GPTYE	________________
NGAOAL	________ ________	WADRNA	________________
TZIAAANN	________________	GEALRIA	________________
ENKYA	________________	ANGHA	________________
MLIAASO	________________	HIEPIATO	________________
LAIM	________________	DASUN	________________
MBBWZIAE	________________	DAGAMASCAR	________________
MCCROOO	________________	DAGAUN	________________

Answers: Chad, Liberia, South Africa, Angola, Tanzania, Kenya, Somalia, Mali, Zimbabwe, Morocco, Senegal, Nigeria, Egypt, Rwanda, Algeria, Ghana, Ethiopia, Sudan, Madagascar, Uganda

Notable People Scramble

Unscramble the last names of the faces below. Write the answers in the word wheel around the picture of each person.

1. Lorraine ________________ NSHARRYBE
   Hint: This famous playwright wrote *A Raisin in the Sun* in 1959.
2. Jean Baptiste __________ _____ __________ NIPTO UD BLESA
   Hint: This Black pioneer founded a settlement which later became Chicago!
3. Leotyne ____________ CEPIR
   Hint: This Black opera singer once received a 42 minute ovation!
4. Mahalia ______________ CKJAONS
   Hint: This gospel singer sold 1 million copies of her first album!
5. Chief Charles ________________ ASONDERN
   Hint: this famous Black pilot helped train America's first Black fighter pilots.

NAME BANK
Anderson
Price
Jackson
Hansberry
Point du Sable

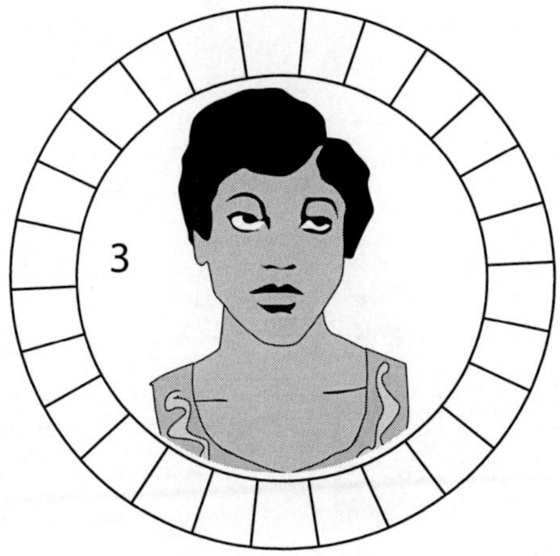

Answers: 1. Hansberry, 2. Point du Sable, 3. Price, 4. Jackson, 5. Anderson

Kwanzaa Spelling Bee

Good spelling is a good habit! Study the words on the page. Most all of them can be found within the activities in this book! Then fold the right half of the page under. Take a "spelling test!" Ask a friend to read the words aloud to you. Write the correct spelling on the line. When finished, unfold the page and check your spelling. How many did you spell right? Study the words you miss.

WORDS

____________________	Kwanzaa
____________________	ancestor
____________________	creativity
____________________	symbol
____________________	heritage
____________________	rejoice
____________________	determination
____________________	celebrate
____________________	Africa
____________________	unity
____________________	present
____________________	cooperation
____________________	faith
____________________	future
____________________	principle
____________________	struggle
____________________	remember
____________________	purpose
____________________	responsibility

The Underground Railroad

Harriet Tubman helped hundreds of enslaved people escape toward the North for freedom. They traveled on the "Underground Railroad." The "railroad" was a network of homes owned by people who helped those escaping slavery. Harriet also helped the Union Army during the Civil War. She was a spy!

The "friendly" houses below are marked with letters. Starting in the South, follow the trail to find the secret word. Color the friendly houses.

Two Make One

Match the first and last names of these famous African Americans. On a separate sheet of paper, write the reason why each person is famous.

1	Jean Baptiste	________	King Jr.
2	Countee	________	Jackson
3	Rosa	________	Morrison
4	George Washington	________	Cullen
5	Arthur	________	Parks
6	Jesse	________	Truth
7	Martin Luther	________	Ashe
8	Dr. Charles	________	Point du Sable
9	Barack	________	Owens
10	Mahalia	________	Drew
11	Toni	________	Carver
12	Sojourner	________	Obama

Answers: Jean Baptiste Point du Sable, 2. Countee Cullen, 3. Rosa Parks, 4. George Washington Carver, 5. Arthur Ashe, 6. Jesse Owens, 7. Martin Luther King, Jr., 8. Dr. Charles Drew, 9. Barack Obama, 10. Mahalia Jackson, 11. Toni Morrison, 12. Sojourner Truth

Stewing in the Kitchen!

Enslaved Black women became cooks in kitchens across the South. They brought many new recipes and different foods from Africa to America. Black women had to use all their resources when the pantry grew bare. They looked to nature to find some of their ingredients. Here are a few different recipes to try in your classroom or at home with a parent.

Okra is native to tropical Africa and Asia. Okra arrived in America with the slave trade.

Fried Okra

1 lb. of fresh okra (cut in 1/4-inch rounds)
1 &1/2 cups corn meal
1/3 cup oil
Salt, pepper

Salt and pepper okra, then shake it in a brown paper sack with 1 & 1/2 cups of cornmeal until okra is all covered. Heat skillet very hot with 1/3 cup of oil. Put in okra and fry to golden brown (12 minutes or thereabout). Remove from skillet and lay okra on paper towel to absorb excess oil. Serve hot. Enough for 4 hungry people.

Pralines

2 cups light brown sugar
2 cups granulated sugar
1/2 tsp. baking soda
2 tsp. vanilla
1 cup pecans (whole)
2 tablespoons white syrup
1 small can evaporated milk
1 cup water
2 tablespoons butter

Blend together milk, water, soda, and syrup. Blend well or milk will curdle. Stir in mixed brown and white sugar. Cook to "soft ball" stage. Remove from fire and beat until light brown. Put in vanilla, then butter and, last, pecans. Drop on wax paper and let cool. Makes about 24 medium-large patties.

Pull Apart Facts

"Pull apart" these sentences to discover cool trivia about African Americans! Write your answer on the lines provided.

1. ShirleyFranklin,mayorofAtlanta,wasthefirstAfricanAmericanfemale mayorofamajorSouthernU.S.city.

____

____

____

2. Itwasagainstthelawtoteachanenslavedpersontoreadorwriteduringthe yearsofslaveryinAmerica,butmanylearnedinsecret.

____

____

____

3. BayardRustinorganizedthe1963MarchonWashington,whereMartin LutherKing,Jr.deliveredhisfamous"IHaveADream"speechattheLincoln Memorialtoacrowdofthousands.

____

____

____

4. U.S.ArmyinterpreterIsaiahDormandiedwithGeneralCusterin1876atthe BattleofLittleBigHorn.

____

____

____

Amazing Firsts!

Use the Word Wheel to fill in the blanks.

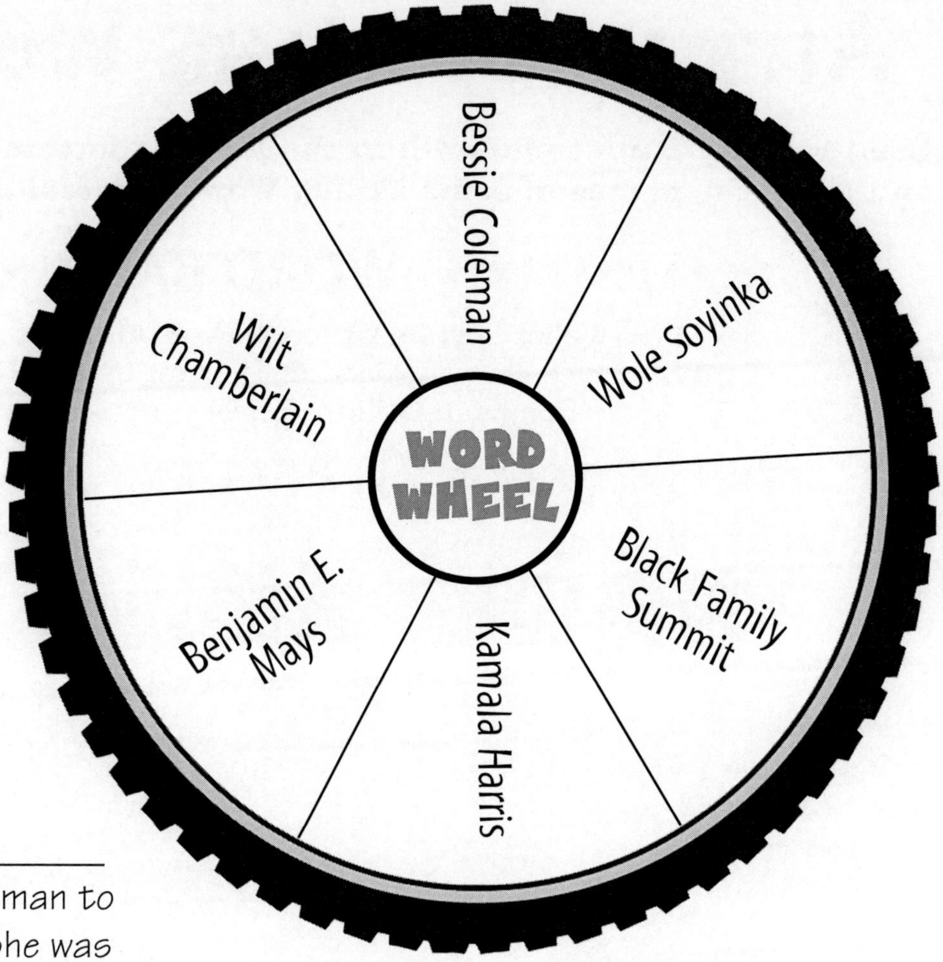

1. In November 2020, ________________ became the first female, African American, and Asian American to become Vice President of the United States.

2. In 1921, ______________________ became the first Black woman to receive a pilot's license. She was also the first Black woman stunt pilot.

3. The first ______________________ took place at Fisk University, Tennessee, in May 1984.

4. ______________________ was the first professional basketball player to score more than 3,000 points in one season and the first Black player to score 100 points in a single game.

5. In 1967, ______________________ was elected the first Black president of the Atlanta Public School Board of Education.

6. In 1986, Nigerian playwright, poet, and novelist ______________________ became the first African to win a Nobel Prize for literature.

Answers: Kamala Harris, Bessie Coleman, Black Family Summit, Wilt Chamberlain, Benjamin E. Mays, Wole Soyinka

African Americans Word Wizards

Use the Word Bank to help fill in the missing letters and learn the names of some skilled Word Wizards!

WORD BANK

Alice Walker, fiction writer ● William Wells Brown, novelist
Paul Laurence Dunbar, poet ● William Cooper Nell, historical writer
Benjamin Griffith Brawley, non-fiction author

_ A U L   L A _ R _ N C _
D U N B _ R

Swahili is the most widely spoken language in Africa.

More than 1,000 different languages are spoken in Africa.

B E _ J A _ I N
G _ I _ F I T H   _ R A W L _ Y

_ I _ L I A M
C _ O P _ R   N E _ L

A _ I C E   _ A L _ E R

South Africa has 11 official languages.

W _ L L I _ M
W _ L L S   B R _ W N

Answers: Paul Laurence Dunbar, Benjamin Griffith Brawley, William Cooper Nell, Alice Walker, William Wells Brown

Wildlife Matching

Match the animals, which are all native to Africa, with their correct pictures. Color the animals.

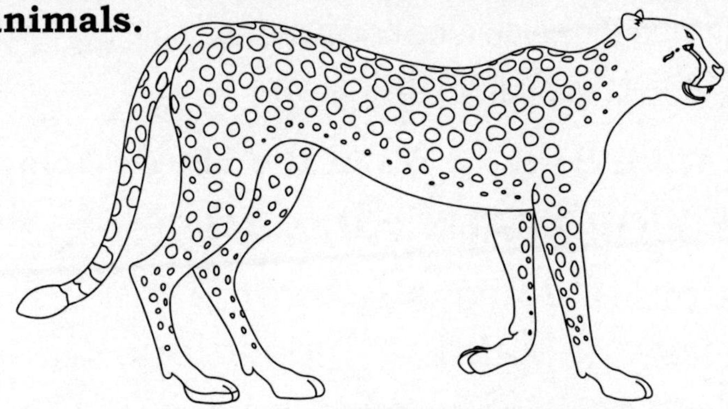

Cheetah

Buffalo

Lion

Gazelle

Penguin

Swan

Frog

Crocodile

Elephant

Giraffe

Hyena

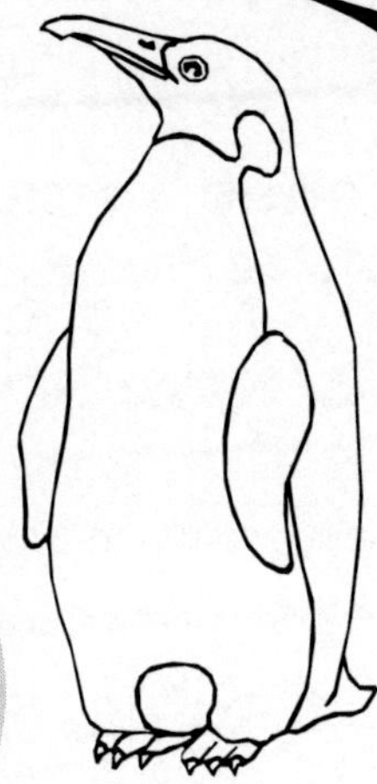

Cheetahs are the fastest land animals on earth. They can run between 60 and 70 miles per hour!

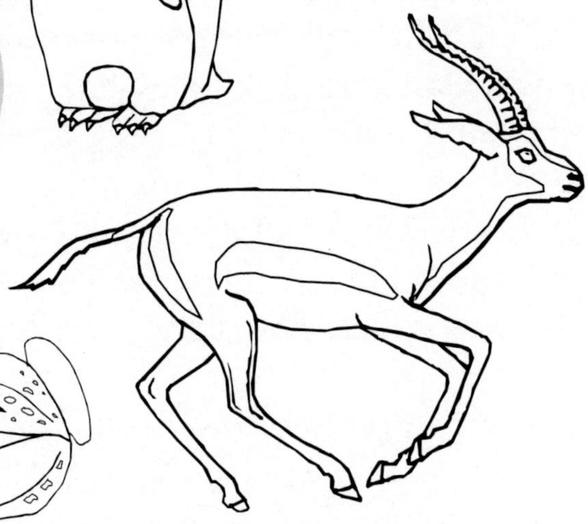

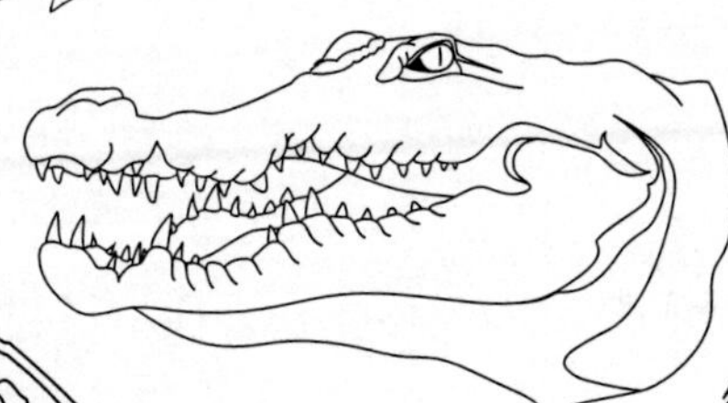

Black Americans Overcame Obstacles

Many famous African Americans overcame tremendous obstacles to achieve great things. They did not allow other people to decide who they would be or what they could do. These people decided that no one would distract them from their goals.

Read each question. Use the Word Bank to fill in the blanks below.

WORD BANK

money	orators	Cross	woman
nurse	slavery	land	positions

1. Shirley Franklin served in many different city government __________ before Atlanta citizens elected her mayor in 2002. She waited a long time to become mayor, but chose to stay busy learning her whole life. Franklin was the first African American _________ to serve as mayor of a major city in the South.

2. Frederick Douglass did not have the opportunity to attend school, like many children do today, because he was enslaved. He found a way to save __________ and was finally able to buy his freedom.

3. Amos Fortune was enslaved for a long time. He worked hard, saved his _________ and was finally able to buy his freedom. Fortune eventually bought the freedom of his wife and saved enough to buy his own plot of _________.

4. Susie King Taylor decided that she wanted to become a __________ like Clara Barton, founder of the American Red _______. She wanted to help the Black soldiers who were wounded in the Civil War. Taylor served until the war ended.

Choose two goals you want to achieve. Write one thing you can do to help you meet each goal.

Goal	How to Prepare
______________________	______________________
______________________	______________________

Answers: 1. positions, woman; 2. slavery, orators; 3. money 4. nurse, Cross

Juneteenth Crossword

On June 19, 1865, **WSNE** ________________ of the Emancipation Proclamation signed by President Abraham Lincoln finally arrived in Texas, after two-and-a-half years! Major General Gordon Granger read an official announcement in Galveston, Texas, and then **SAEVLDNE** ________________ people were **EEFR** ________________ ! Everyone joined in a joyous celebration full of praying, feasting, dancing, and singing!

Today Juneteenth is an unofficial **LIHAYOD** ________________ . When formerly enslaved people from **ASTEX** ________________ migrated, they spread this **JETUENTNEH** ________________ tradition around the United States. It has become a holiday across the country.

WORD BANK

free Texas Juneteenth
enslaved news holiday

Unscramble the words in the paragraphs above. Then use the Word Bank to solve the crossword puzzle.

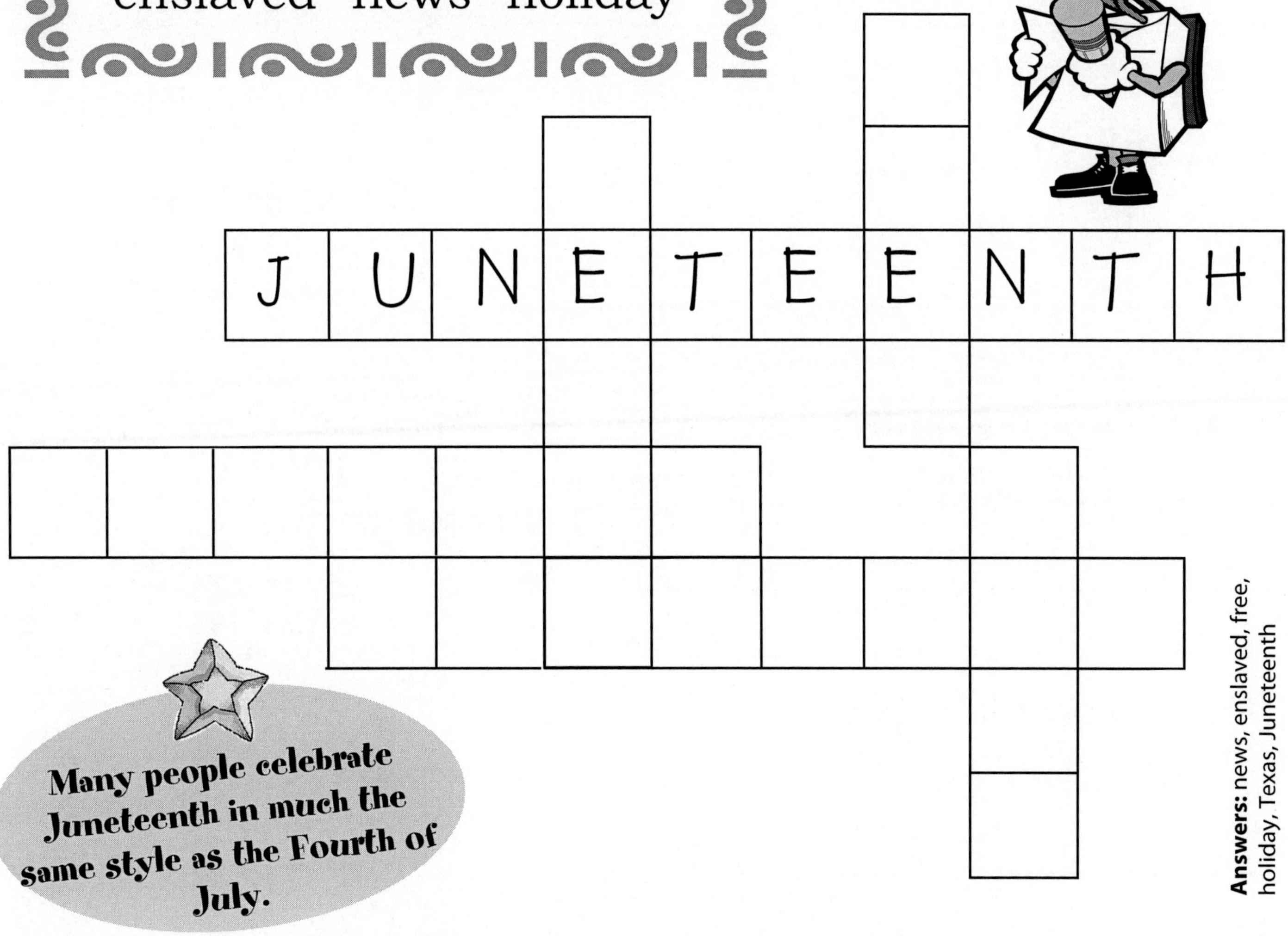

Many people celebrate Juneteenth in much the same style as the Fourth of July.

Answers: news, enslaved, free, holiday, Texas, Juneteenth

Mirror, Mirror On the Wall

Swahili is an African language. Find the meaning of each Swahili word by holding this page up to a mirror. Write the meanings on the lines provided.

IMANI **(*ee*-MAH-*nee*)**

believing in yourself

____

KUUMBA **(koo-OO-mbah)**

a new way to do something

____

NIA **(NEE-ah)**

purposeful living

____

UJIMA **(*oo*-JEE-mah)**

working together

____

UMOJA **(*oo*-MOH-jah)**

unity

____

PRONUNCIATIONS

a = *ah* as in *father*
e = *a* as in *day*
i = *ee* as in *free*
o = *o* as in *go*
u = *oo* as in *too*

Buzzing Around Black Athletes!

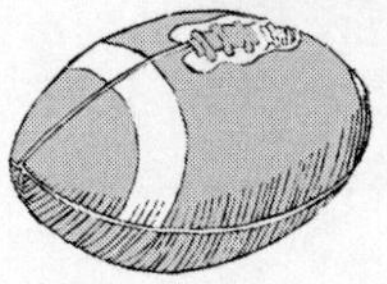

African Americans also show their talent in the professional sports arena. Black athletes participate in basketball, soccer, football, baseball, gymnastics, tennis, and other sports!

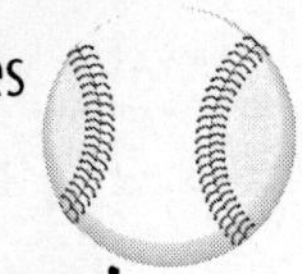

Find the answers to the questions by buzzing through the maze!

1. Black basketball star ______________ ______________________ helped the Chicago Bulls win 5 NBA championships!
2. The first African American to play baseball in the major leagues was ______________ __________________! He played for the Brooklyn Dodgers.
3. African American sisters ___________________ and _____________________ ____________________________ play professional tennis!
4. Gymnast _____________ __________________ flipped her way to Olympic greatness!
5. Riding jockey ____________________ _________________________ rode a horse named Aristides in the Kentucky Derby!
6. Chicago Bears running back ____________________ _________________________ is remembered as one of the greatest football players of all time!
7. African American boxer _________________________ __________________ floated like a butterfly and stung like a bee.
8. WNBA Black basketball star ___________________ _______________________ was named both WNBA Most Valuable Player and Defensive Player of the Year in 2000.

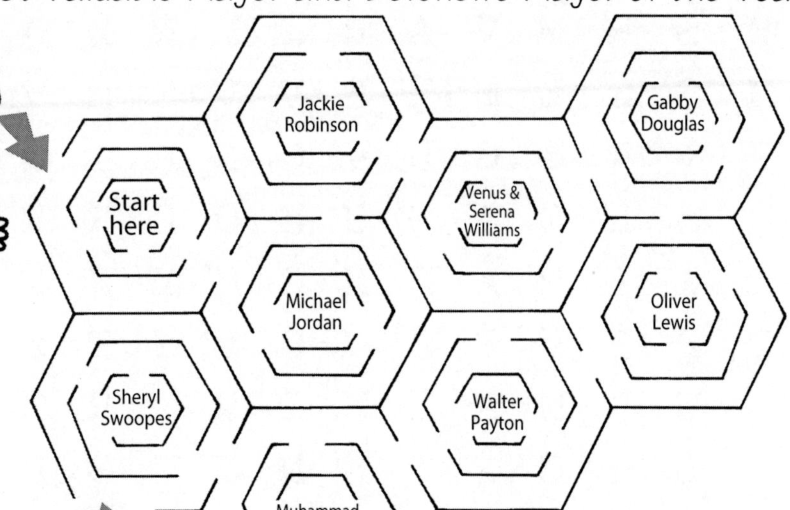

Answers: 1. Michael Jordan, 2. Jackie Robinson, 3. Venus and Serena Williams, 4. Gabby Douglas, 5. Oliver Lewis, 6. Walter Payton, 7. Muhammad Ali, 8. Sheryl Swoopes

Collegiate Word Search

Many historically Black colleges and universities educate students in the United States. Here are some examples of great schools that teach students how to succeed in today's world.

Find the words.

Word Bank

Howard University	Tuskegee University	Spelman College
Stillman College	Morehouse College	Shaw University
Selma University	Bennett College	Fisk University
Lincoln University	Morris Brown College	

T	Y	Z	B	R	U	E	R	K	Z	R	E	Z	X	W	S	E	L	E	S	M
H	U	T	I	Y	Z	S	S	F	K	B	Y	Y	F	S	Y	I	S	G	P	O
I	X	S	I	N	H	D	G	K	E	Y	Q	C	H	Q	N	E	J	E	E	R
E	H	Y	K	S	X	L	W	D	S	D	U	A	Z	C	G	T	J	L	L	R
G	G	F	S	E	R	M	Z	B	F	F	W	K	O	E	B	P	Y	L	M	I
S	W	B	A	K	G	E	K	Y	F	U	Q	L	L	M	U	O	Y	O	A	S
S	W	H	G	R	N	E	V	B	N	B	N	L	G	D	O	V	I	C	N	B
D	G	T	P	K	K	R	E	I	V	U	O	T	H	J	E	X	S	E	C	R
V	T	J	W	E	S	W	V	U	N	C	G	K	F	B	Y	T	W	S	O	O
C	Y	T	I	S	R	E	V	I	N	U	D	R	A	W	O	H	F	U	L	W
D	K	W	E	S	R	M	V	A	H	I	K	W	Z	A	Y	L	X	O	L	N
J	T	V	M	S	Z	E	M	H	H	F	V	S	M	V	R	H	R	H	E	C
D	N	T	I	V	R	L	G	N	V	O	N	E	I	N	S	P	X	E	G	O
I	M	T	U	S	L	S	A	M	U	E	O	L	R	F	L	S	K	R	E	L
M	Y	V	I	I	I	R	X	H	X	G	M	Y	H	S	M	U	D	O	H	L
U	C	T	T	P	Z	V	E	J	G	O	L	G	T	Z	I	R	L	M	W	E
S	Y	S	S	E	L	M	A	U	N	I	V	E	R	S	I	T	Y	K	N	G
E	G	E	L	L	O	C	T	T	E	N	N	E	B	B	E	C	Y	K	N	E
R	H	Y	W	C	Z	J	I	N	J	J	B	J	W	B	S	O	F	M	E	C
A	F	V	U	J	H	R	H	V	G	D	J	Q	Q	P	L	G	O	U	H	W

Send Me!

The United States Postal Service issues new stamps each year. Some stamps honor great Americans.

Choose a great African American! Design a stamp to honor his or her achievements. Write some of this person's contributions to America.

Name ____

Contributions ____

____

Flag Find!

How many bendera flags can you find in this picture? Write your answer in the box. Color the picture.

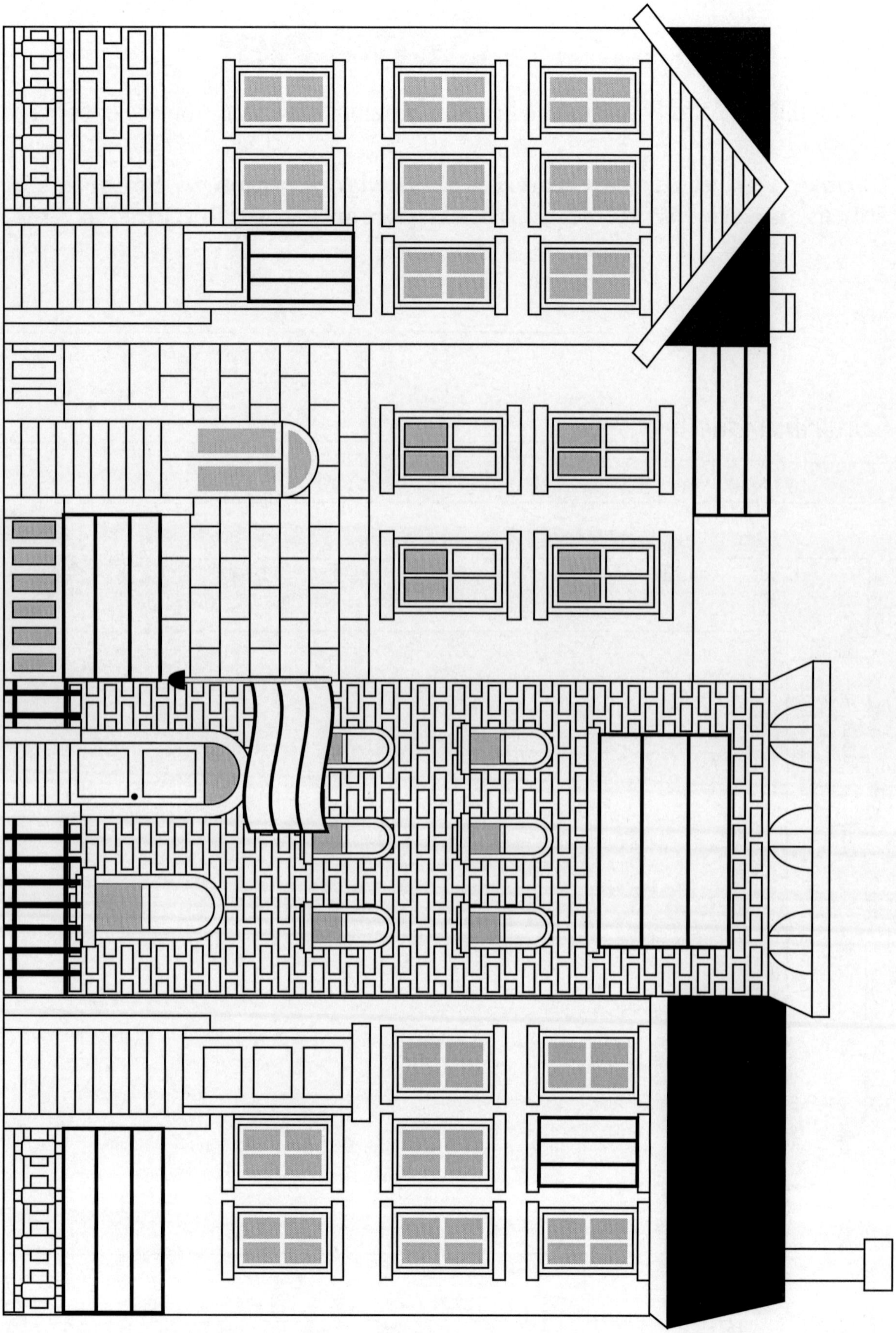

Answer: 7

Color Me!

BLUE
Blue like the uniforms that Black Union soldiers wore in the Civil War
Blue
YELLOW
Yellow like the dawning of a new day for civil rights
Yellow
RED
Red like the brightly lit candles at Kwanzaa
Red
African
American
Light Brown
LIGHT BROWN
Light brown like the peanuts George Washington Carver used for experiments
Purple
PURPLE
Purple like the beautiful quilts that enslaved women sewed
Green
GREEN
Green like the forests where enslaved people traveled on their journey to freedom

African Geo-Facts

Read these fascinating tidbits of information about African geography. Underline each noun and circle each verb.

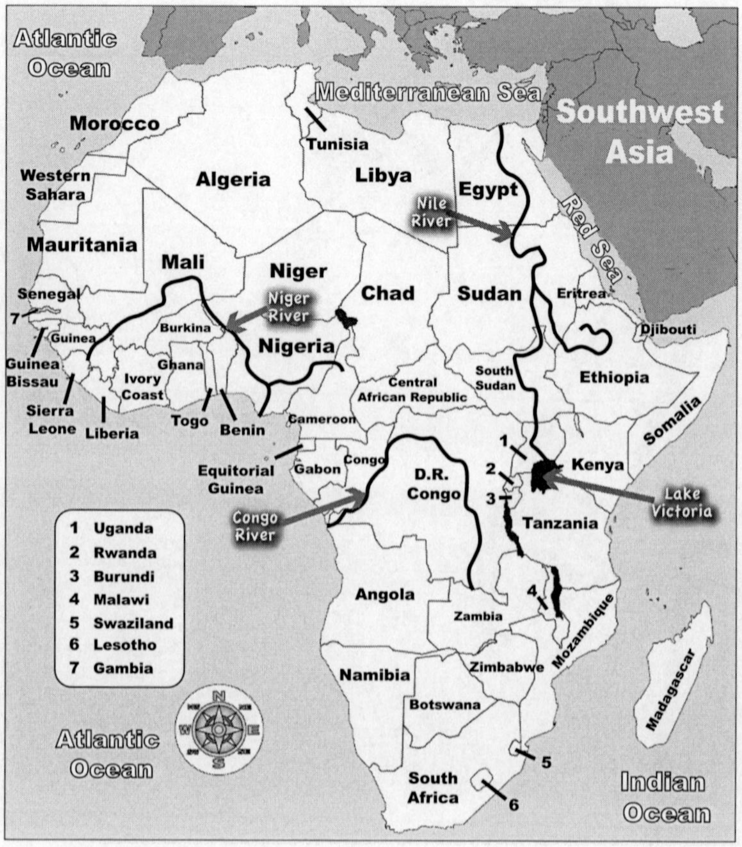

- Africa is the second largest continent on Earth. It covers about 11,699,000 square miles (30,330,000 square km)!
- Algeria, located in northwestern Africa, is the largest country on the African continent. Seychelles is the smallest African country.
- Mount Kilimanjaro in Tanzania is the highest point in Africa. Lake Assal in Djibouti is the lowest point.
- The northernmost tip is Cape Blanc in Tunisia, and the southernmost tip is Cape Agulhas in South Africa.
- Lake Victoria is the largest lake in Africa and the world's second largest freshwater lake. Lake Tanganyika is the deepest lake in Africa; its greatest depth is 4,710 feet (1,436 m).
- The Nile, which drains northeastern Africa, is the longest river in Africa and in the world.
- The Namib Desert is the world's oldest desert.
- The Fish River Canyon in Namibia is the second largest canyon in the world.
- The Sahara Desert is expanding southward each year.

Birmingham Civil Rights Institute

The Birmingham Civil Rights Institute is a museum and educational center in Birmingham, Alabama that exhibits the fight for civil rights in the United States and beyond. The journey includes the era of segregation, the Civil Rights Movement of the 1950s and 1960s, and the worldwide struggle for civil and human rights. The Institute's projects and services involve research and encourage discussion on human rights in America and around the world.

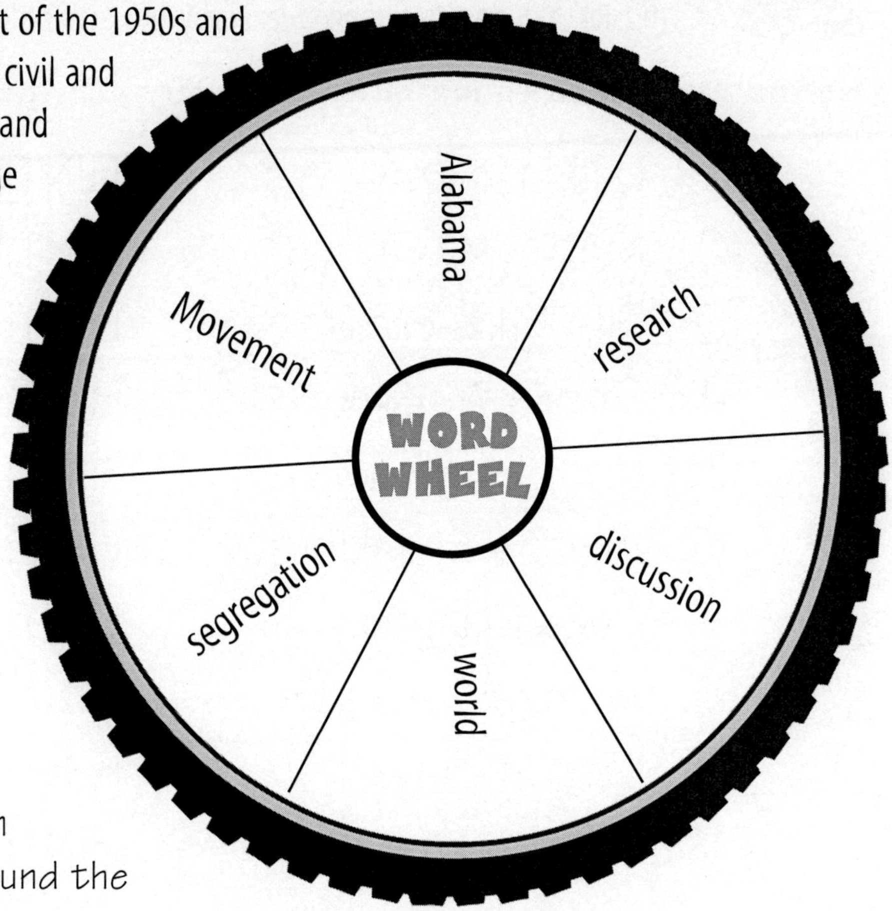

Use the Word Wheel to fill in the blanks.

1. The Birmingham Civil Rights Institute promotes ______________ about civil and human rights.

2. The museum features exhibits about civil rights in the United States and around the ________________.

3. The Birmingham Civil Rights Institute is located in Birmingham, ____________.

4. Scholars at the Institute continue to learn about civil rights through ____________.

5. One major exhibit at the museum describes the era of ________________.

6. The Civil Rights ________________ took place during the 1950s and 1960s.

Answers: 1. discussion, 2. world, 3. Alabama, 4. research, 5. segregation, 6. Movement

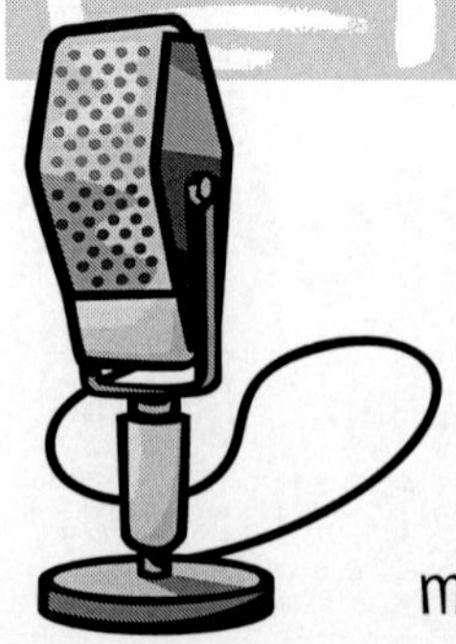

Own the Microphone!

African American musicians have created new twists with soulful, energetic songs throughout the decades. Black voices can be heard loud and proud in every type of music; they have influenced jazz, rhythm and blues, rap, swing, soul, and funk!

Use the Word Bank to match each singer with the correct song.

	Singer		Hint
______	1. Billie Holiday	HINT:	Rain, snow, sleet...
______	2. Run-D.M.C.	HINT:	Which direction?
______	3. Ella Fitzgerald	HINT:	You crack me up!
______	4. Stevie Wonder	HINT:	Not twice!
______	5. Nat "King" Cole	HINT:	I never forget a face.
______	6. Aretha Franklin	HINT:	All I want is a little...
______	7. Duke Ellington	HINT:	Twirl around!
______	8. Michael Jackson	HINT:	Rhymes with chiller!
______	9. Marvin Gaye	HINT:	What's happening?
______	10. Louis Armstrong	HINT:	Earth rocks!

ANSWER BANK

(A) For Once In My Life
(B) What's Going On
(C) Respect
(D) Stormy Weather
(E) Thriller
(F) Unforgettable
(G) My Funny Valentine
(H) Walk This Way
(I) What A Wonderful World
(J) It Don't Mean A Thing, If It Ain't Got that Swing

Answers: 1.D, 2.H, 3.G, 4.A, 5.F, 6.C, 7.J, 8.E, 9.B, 10.I

State Shapes!

Look at the pictures to answer each question. Write your answer on the line. Color each picture.

1. Which state legalized slavery in 1661?

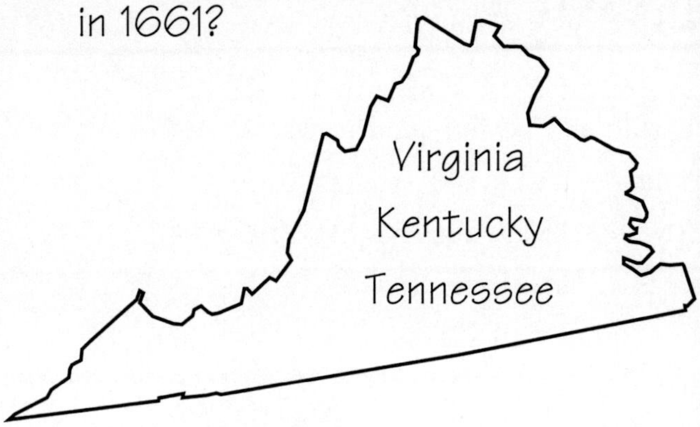

Virginia
Kentucky
Tennessee

____

2. In which state is the African American community of Harlem located?

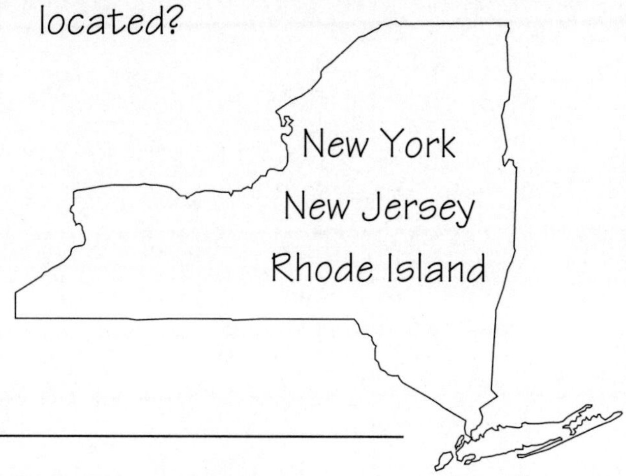

New York
New Jersey
Rhode Island

____

3. In which country was the NAACP (National Association for the Advancement of Colored People) founded?

Canada
United States
Mexico

____

4. Where did the March on Washington take place in 1963?

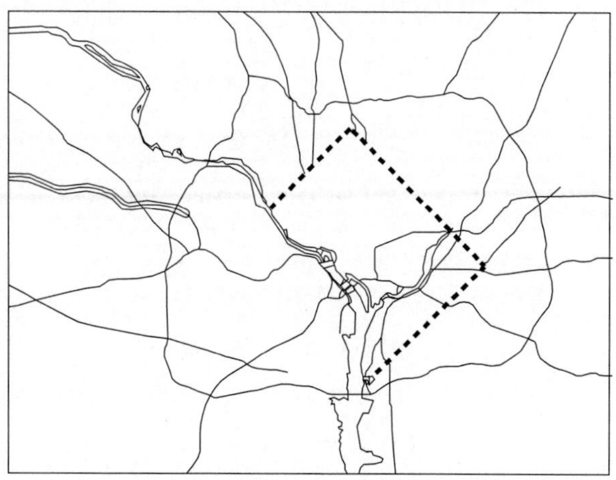

Washington • California
Washington, D.C.

____

Answers: 1. Virginia, 2. New York, 3. Canada, 4. Washington, D.C.

The History of Kwanzaa

Read the story. Highlight all the nouns yellow.
Underline all the verbs in red.

Once there was a man named Maulana Karenga. He was a very intelligent African American scholar. Maulana looked around his world and saw racial inequality, the battle for civil rights, and prejudice. He believed that African Americans needed to learn more about their African history. He knew that Africans would unite into a stronger community if they understood and honored their common ancestry.

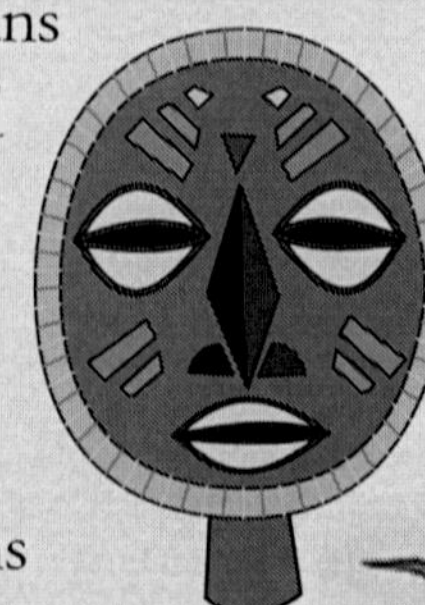

In 1966, Maulana Karenga decided to combine many different African customs and traditions into one special holiday called Kwanzaa. The word Kwanzaa means "first fruits" in Swahili, an African language. Many families all around the world observe Kwanzaa, an African American holiday celebrated for seven days, from December 26 to January 1.

The celebration of Kwanzaa focuses on Seven Principles (*Nguzo Saba*). These principles are taught by using the Seven Symbols. Families spread the *mkeka* on a low table. The *kinara* and *kikombe cha umoja* are placed in the center. The *muhindi* are placed around the *kinara*. The *mishumaa saba* are set to the far right. The *zawadi* and *mazao* go on the *mkeka*. The symbols and principles are designed to pull the African American community together and to grow stronger as one body.

Code Red! Revolt!

Solve the codes to learn the names of famous enslaved people who led rebellions in the early 1800s.

A	B	C	D	E	F	G	H	I	J	K	L	M
✹	❁	✣	♣	➳	♥	❢	✻	✄	✆	☛	✈	✉

N	O	P	Q	R	S	T	U	V	W	X	Y	Z
✿	✪	✦	✡	✎	❦	☎	✒	✚	✖	✍	✠	✓

___ ___ ___ ___ ___ ___ ___   ___ ___ ___ ___ ___ ___ ___

❢ ✹ ❁ ✎ ✄ ➳ ✈   ✦ ✎ ✪ ❦ ❦ ➳ ✎

___ ___ ___   ___ ___ ___ ___ ___ ___

✿ ✹ ☎   ☎ ✒ ✎ ✿ ➳ ✎

___ ___ ___ ___ ___ ___ ___   ___ ___ ___ ___ ___ ___

♣ ➳ ✿ ✉ ✹ ✎ ☛   ✚ ➳ ❦ ➳ ❦ ✠

The largest rebellion of enslaved people in U.S. history took place in present-day Louisiana in 1811. At the time, Louisiana was not yet a state. The revolt was known as the German Coast Uprising.

Answers: Gabriel Prosser, Nat Turner, Denmark Vesey

Order In The Court!

African American history is full of important court cases and new laws. These cases and new laws helped change the treatment of African Americans.

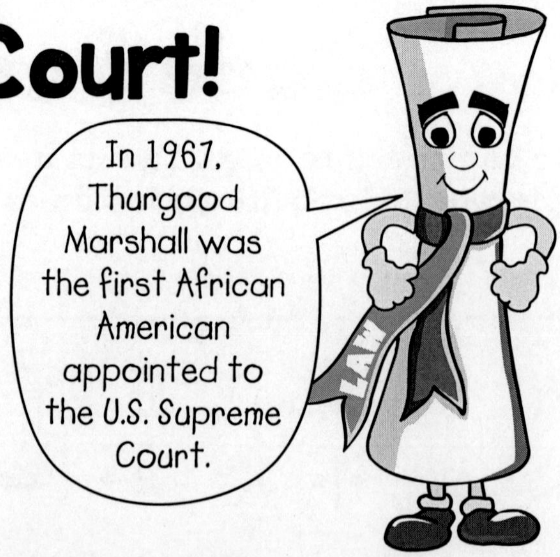

Order! Order! Order in the court! These dates are all mixed up! Number the events on the timeline in chronological order.

_______ U.S. Supreme Court declares segregated public schools unconstitutional in the *Brown vs. Board of Education* court case. (1954)

_______ Enslaved Virginian Dred Scott sues for his freedom (and his family's freedom) on the grounds that his master had moved to a free state. The U.S. Supreme Court rules against him. (1846)

_______ Equal Employment Opportunity Act passes, reducing job discrimination against people of all races, religions, and genders in the United States. (1972)

_______ Congress passes the Voting Rights Act, which allows Black citizens to vote freely and unhindered. (1965)

_______ U.S. Supreme Court legalizes separate but equal facilities for Black and white people in the *Plessy vs. Ferguson* court case. (1896)

Answers: 3, 1, 5, 4, 2

Notable Black Doctors!

• One of the first Black people in America known to work with medicine was the enslaved Black man Oneisimus who developed an antidote for smallpox.

• Dr. Theodore Lawless helped thousands who suffered from various skin ailments. He also taught medicine at Northwestern University, his alma mater, for more than fifteen years.

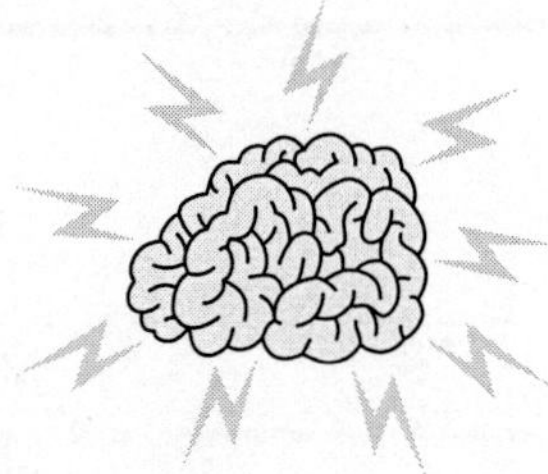

• Doctor Rebecca Lee was one of the first Black doctors in the United States.

• Dr. James Durham was the first Black doctor in America.

• Dr. Ulysses Grant Dailey was known for his skill in the operating room.

• Dr. Daniel Hale Williams performed the world's first successful open-heart operation in 1893. Dr. Williams also founded the Black Provident Hospital in Chicago, Illinois and the first Black nursing school in Washington, D.C.

Match the Black doctors below with their most notable medical accomplishment!

1. Dr. Theodore Lawless
2. Dr. Ulysses Grant Dailey
3. Dr. Daniel Hale Williams
4. Dr. Rebecca Lee
5. Oneisimus
6. Dr. James Durham

A. one of world's leading dermatologists
B. first Black female to earn a medical degree
C. performed first successful open heart surgery in the world
D. enslaved man who developed smallpox antidote
E. first American Black doctor
F. skilled Black surgeon

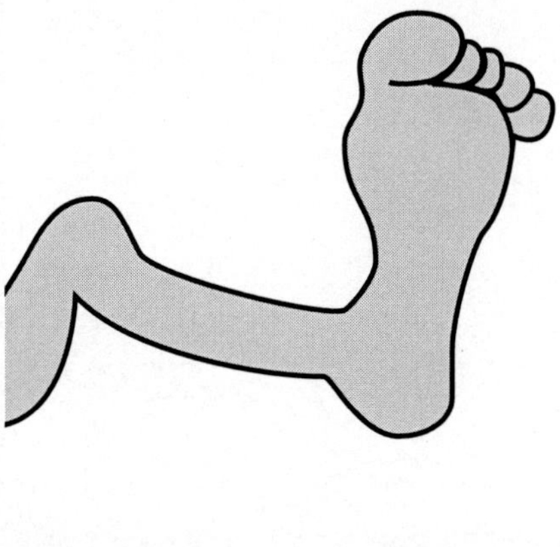

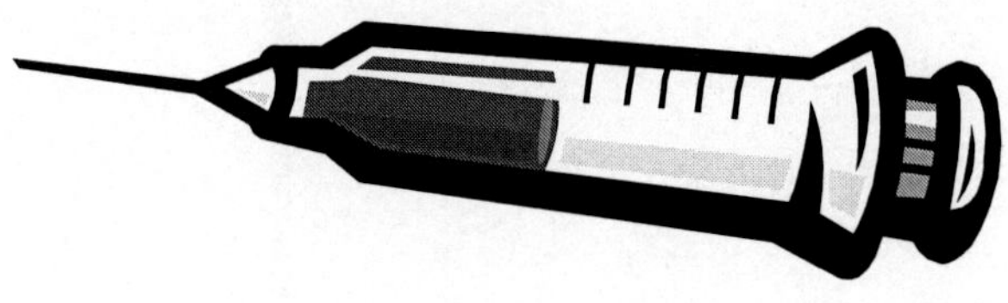

Answers: 1.A, 2.F, 3.C, 4.B, 5.D, 6.E

Scrapbook of...

Check out these pictures of African American events in history. Are you familiar with all of them? Research some more events and draw them in the spaces provided. Create your own scrapbook of African American history!

Use the blank boxes to get started.

Martin Luther King Jr. delivering his famous "I Have a Dream" speech, Washington, D.C. (1963)

16th Street Baptist Church, Birmingham, AL

African American Soldiers Monument, Chicago, IL

African American History

Howard University
Washington, D.C. (1979)

Jackie Robinson at bat for the Brooklyn Dodgers,
New York City (1954)

Frederick Douglass House, Wash., D.C. (1963)

Abolitionist Crossword

Use the Word Bank to solve the crossword puzzle.

WORD BANK

North free orator Lincoln illegal

ACROSS

1. Many abolitionists worked to make slavery ________________.
2. Frederick Douglass was a famous ________________ who delivered speeches against slavery.

DOWN

3. Black abolitionists Frederick Douglass and Sojourner Truth both advised President Abraham ______________ on how to improve the treatment of Black people.
4. The Emancipation Proclamation of 1863 set enslaved people __________.
5. Two newspapers, Freedom's Journal and the ________________ Star, published articles about the evils of slavery.

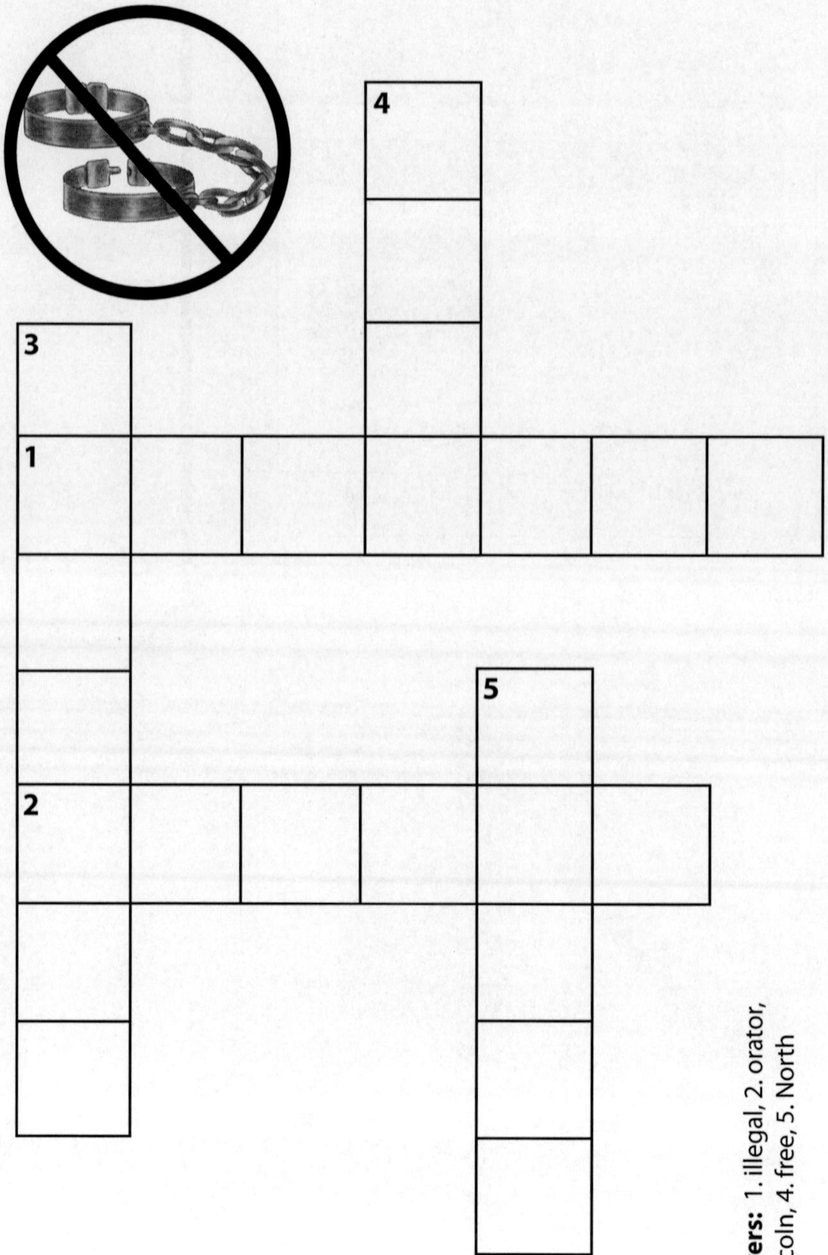

Answers: 1. illegal, 2. orator, 3. Lincoln, 4. free, 5. North

Amazing African Americans!

Acrostic poems are composed by writing a word or phrase that starts with each letter of a word. See if you can write your own acrostic poem about African Americans.

Next to every letter, write a word or phrase that describes African American people. The first letter is done for you. Now let's see what you can do!

A is for Around the Nation!

F is for ____________________

R is for ____________________

I is for ____________________

C is for ____________________

A is for ____________________

N is for ____________________

A is for ____________________

M is for ____________________

E is for ____________________

R is for ____________________

I is for ____________________

C is for ____________________

A is for ____________________

N is for ____________________

Official

BLACK HERITAGE BIG ACTIVITY BOOK

Certificate

Presented to:

____

This certificate verifies that the above named is officially an intellectual of The African American Experience!

Signature ____________________ Date ____________________